Pastoral Prayers For All Seasons

Rolland R. Reece

CSS Publishing Company, Inc., Lima, Ohio

PASTORAL PRAYERS FOR ALL SEASONS

Library of Congress Cataloging-in-Publication Data

Reece, Rolland R., 1927-
    Pastoral prayers for all seasons / Rolland R. Reece.
        p.   cm.
    Includes index.
    ISBN 0-7880-1567-2 (paperback : alk. paper)
    1. Pastoral prayers.   I. Title.
BV250 R44   2000
264'.13—dc21   99-053306

This book is available in the following formats, listed by ISBN:
    0-7880-1567-2   Book
    0-7880-1568-0   Disk
    0-7880-1569-9   Sermon Prep

PRINTED IN U.S.A.

To my wife, Martha

Table Of Contents

The prayers are arranged in keeping with the Church Year. There are also prayers for selected secular days and national holidays.

Introduction

In the beginning years of my ministry, I thought it a good practice to offer Sunday's pastoral prayer extemporaneously. This was the tradition of my boyhood church and it suggested to me a freedom of word and thought. However, after several years of such prayers I became aware that I was using the same words, repeating the same phrases, and addressing the same concerns.

At first — to break up these patterns — I began using a sparse outline, but gradually it became more and more "fleshed out." Finally I was writing the entire prayer.

It was always a challenge to determine what the subject(s) of a prayer should be. Imaginatively, and sometimes literally, I would place myself in a pew to obtain a sense of what the congregation wished to bring to God's attention. After determining the theme, a greater struggle may appear — getting started. One of my resources for getting "unstuck" was the use of books of prayers written by other pastors. Rarely did I use another pastor's prayer as my own. But frequently I found a phrase, a sentence, or an idea that would trigger my creativity, which in turn would jump-start the writing of the congregational prayer. It is my intention that the prayers of this book will serve other pastors and worship leaders in the same way.

Rolland R. Reece

Advent/Christmas Seasons

Advent

Christmas Eve/Christmas Day

New Year's Eve

1 We're starting on a journey to reach Bethlehem, O God. We know where it is in modern day Israel — at least we think we do — and we know something of the preparations needed to get there. But it isn't the Bethlehem in Israel we seek, it's the Bethlehem of our faith, the one that requires an inner journey. The one we can reach only because we have a growing faith in you. The day of our arrival is called Christmas.

Much distracts us. Much discourages us. Much misleads us. It is easier to go with the flow, to follow along from one place or event to another, killing time, with the knowledge that eventually this Christmas — like those before it — will run its course. And then we won't have to think or feel.

But if we would take a different tack, even a slightly different one, what would become of us? And of those we love? And of those we don't love? We really do want to break through all the layers of tradition and merriment to reach your Son personally. We want to come into the presence of him who spent his life in our behalf. We want to know a love that stands up to the worst of defeats, a love that rises victoriously over all the elements of our lives that, otherwise, would carry us to isolation and ruin.

We thank you, God, for your Son who is the one who embodies this love. He is the Bethlehem for which we search. Armed with prayer and scripture we are equipped to find him who holds the key to the abundant life for which we yearn.

We lift our voices in praise to you for the gift of your Son. Hallelujah! Amen.

Advent

2 We wonder, O God, what we would have believed if we had lived in first century Israel. Would we have been convinced that this child, the first born son of Mary and Joseph, was indeed the promised Messiah? Would we have later believed that he died for us — for us! — then rose from the dead, granting us life ever after? Or would we have gone along our usual ways, not bothering ourselves with such questions? Of course we like to think we would have been wise and courageous.

We do know that the birth story of Jesus moves us. Its simplicity and homeliness allows it to slip past any defense or cross-examination we may muster. We readily clasp it to our hearts.

Could we be Joseph — trusting and straightforward? Could we be Mary — bright, eager, and believing? What a beautiful family they make even in that lowly shelter.

Are we too sentimental about this event? Do we read too much joy and happiness into it? Because we want it to be such a magnificent moment, do we fashion it from our pastel-colored fantasies and let reality be hung?

Indeed it does play upon our emotions. Even in the jam-packed business of our lives we recognize our need to stop and take into our hearts this compelling event of trust and love. Whatever else is true, this is the stuff of which life is made. If we overlook this event, we are convinced we will have diminished the power of truth. How beautiful the angel voices, "Glory to God in the highest, and on earth peace among men." In the name of our Master we pray. Amen.

3 O God, how grateful we are that you determined to visit us. Your coming has made an indescribable difference in the lives of millions.

However, it surprises us, when we think about it, that you would come as a baby. Many of the great appearances in our lives are made by adults. When a great person comes, the hosts and guests must know where to stand or sit, what words to use in greeting and conversation, what clothes to wear, and what foods to prepare and serve. Scholars are on hand to interpret from one language to another. Reporters hover about taking notes to create the latest news. Then there are the inconspicious ones, body guards, protecting the great person's life.

This is so foreign to the arrival of your Son, Lord. He came in squalor, pain, and fear in the form of a helpless baby. It seems so, well, un-Godlike. The coming of a baby still does not turn our world upside down, far outside the circle of family and friends. A coming of a great person today brings excitement, color, an opportunity for display. It is an occasion to strut, flaunt, and give a wide berth to pride.

A baby, on the other hand, requires responsibility, a need for constant care and love, and a training that leads to sterling character and high morals. These tasks are not nearly so heady and glamorous as tending a great person.

Yet within our hearts, in that quiet place, we wish to cast aside our habitual need to exercise our pride and the ever increasing demands of self, that once fed will always want more. We would die to this self for the truth we find in you and in the helpless baby who is, at last, the way, the truth, and the life. Hear us, our eternal Spirit. Amen.

Advent

4 It is difficult for us, O God, to understand how the people of the first century didn't, or wouldn't, recognize the Messiah. His coming had been taught and explained for centuries; even so, he came nearly unnoticed. Only a tiny band of people was aware of what was taking place — how much we owe them for their faith and courage. Lesser people might have run and hid.

Now it is our turn, creative Spirit, to watch and wait. For centuries the Bible and the church have been proclaiming the return of your Son. The New Testament offers descriptions of the event. It provides us clues to look for in anticipation of that day. However, it also makes it clear that you and you alone know the time and the place — and it is our task to watch and wait. And be ready!

This is not an easy teaching to accept at face value. We keep wondering how Christ's descent from heaven will be done. If he comes through the sky over Europe, how will we see him? And if that dramatic return is only "hype" to keep our interest in the event — then what else should we be looking for? You know that there are many people in the world who shake their heads at our naivete, at our apparent lack of knowledge and sophistication — that we keep believing something that should best be left back in the first century.

We believe; help us through our unbelief. Strengthen our faith to dare the wisdom of humankind. Your Son came once; we believe he will come again. We shall keep our eyes and hearts ready for his return. When everyone else fails, you do not. We take our stand at your side. In the name of Jesus Christ we pray. Amen.

Advent

5 Some time ago, O God, we watched a filmed account of how a badly burned Russian boy was flown to Galveston, Texas. There he received a most extraordinary treatment which, in turn, produced a miraculous recovery. That this journey worked to any degree, was a testimony to the tenacity of many people who were able to work through unbelievable logistical and institutional red tape.

This morning we are aware that because of our great need, you determined to come to us in the person of Jesus. We didn't need to travel to Galveston, or anywhere else. Because of your earthly visit we were given your immediate and powerful presence. Your coming enabled us to cover the ravages of our sin. What a rescue! We can scarcely imagine how you needed to rearrange your nature and the way of your life to fit into the nature and way of our life.

We are immensely grateful. Where would our hearts be this hour if you hadn't come to earth in the birth of your Son? Would we view life with hope and joy? Would we have dared take the less traveled path, if you had not first taken the path to our door?

We open our hearts to you once more to celebrate your coming to earth. We take you into all the nooks and crannies of our days, so pleased that you want to spend yourself in our company. Thank you, Jesus, for becoming Mary's Christ-child. We pray in gratitude through the Holy Spirit. Amen.

6 Now, Almighty God, we are under way with our Christmas activities, wondering how we will accomplish everything. At this point all these activities promise us the certainty of happiness and joy.

But we've been here before, Lord. We've experienced that the luster of this holy day wears off before the day actually appears. We don't know exactly what happens. We get tired, our nerves become frayed, some of our plans go sour. A most trusted recipe fails. Several of our favorite relatives can't make it to the family gathering. Our neighbors get into a fight and the police are called. A loved one dislikes our gift. Suddenly the bottom drops out of our celebration and we can hardly wait until the season has passed. We're sorry, God, we don't mean for it to end this way. Our best effort to create joy misses the mark.

We seek your forgiveness and a new spirit in the celebration of this holy day. Under your guidance we don't need to settle for disaster. Amen.

7 O God, our Creator, who in your Son, Jesus Christ, has brought us to light, hear us as we praise you for the victory you have scored over darkness. Without you we would be people of the shadows — uncertain as to the nature of life and despairing of finding any hope within it.

Your light is our salvation. It guides us along sure paths. It reveals the stumbling blocks that cause us to fall. It makes known to us the resources and strengths that are available to us.

Yet for reasons seldom clear to us, we often choose the darkness. Are we fearful that in the light we will be exposed as inadequate and unacceptable? Have we succumbed to actions and thoughts that embarrass us, therefore we would rather live hidden lives to keep our secrets from view? Are we uncertain that light will grant us all that it promises? While the darkness is treacherous, at least it is familiar.

Grant us courage to embrace the light. Lead us to trust its goodness. We sense that the darkness will ultimately rob life from us; nevertheless, to vault from darkness to light is a giant leap. The change alone makes us anxious. Yet we have seen what the light has done for others. We have watched how it made a new life of one that was empty and chaotic. We are mesmerized. Our hearts beat rapidly with emotion and anticipation of being set free of the blackness that covers our spirit.

Therefore, in a strange mixture of apprehension and hope we present ourselves to the light. May we ever see clearly. May our paths never lead us into shadows. This we pray in the hope that was revealed in your glorious Son, our Lord Jesus Christ. Amen.

Advent

8 We have come together, O God, to rejoice in the birth of your Son. Already we have placed candles in our windows, twinkling lights around our doors, and Madonna and Child stamps on our greeting cards.

When we were younger we entered into all the activities of this season — hour upon hour, task upon task, celebration upon celebration — and we didn't even grow weary. Or at least we didn't notice it. We were sustained by the excitement and expectation of those days. The gifts and cards became more treasured and the decorations became more dazzling with each passing year.

Now we are adults. We tire more easily. Very few elements of our celebration seem as wondrous as yesteryear's. We no longer throw ourselves into the dizzy whirl without caution. We are more tentative and less believing. We have become worried and fearful. We sing "O Little Town of Bethlehem," but its words get lost in the reports of violence of today's world. We read a friend's card that wishes us peace and joy, but in the background the television gives us the latest death count in a bombed village or on cities' streets. The birth of Jesus, what does it mean seen against our killing fields?

First century Bethlehem is far away and our celebrations don't close the gap. Death and destruction are at hand and overwhelm us. As a result we've reduced this humble event to one more children's story, because we no longer take it at face value. We are a desperate people searching for hope. And we're being told — can we believe it? — that it is to be found in a distant stable on a long ago night.

Can it be true that we will find it in the Christ-child? Is it in the tiny hands of your infant Son? Through our imaginations we feel their softness, their warmth, their gentle squeeze. They are so perfectly formed, so willing to trust, so full of promise.

Whoever dreamed back then that those hands would carry the scrolls of the book of Moses, use carpenter's tools, touch the eyes of the blind, or accept nails that fastened them to the cross.

Those tiny hands — now grown to maturity — knock on our door. For every time we fall, they reach out to help us. They wipe away our tears. They caress us in love.

We tremble in fear and they support us. We panic and they calm us. We are directionless and they point the way.

Through these gentle hands we are linked to the source of our meaning. Neither the surprising acceptance of democracy in communistic countries, nor the promise and hope of a summit meeting of world leaders, empowers us as those tiny hands — that free us from fear, enable us to trust in love again, and lead us toward eternal peace.

In the name of Jesus Christ we pray. Amen.

9 Eternal God, we have taken the pain out of the Christmas story. Surely it was there from the outset. There was the pain that Joseph felt when he was told that his betrothed was with child by another. There was the wearing pain Mary experienced riding on a donkey from her village to Bethlehem. There was the pain that both Joseph and Mary experienced in being turned away from the inn and having to settle for a stable in a barn. And there was the horrendous pain Mary suffered in birthing Jesus.

We have taken the pain out of the story, because we can't abide pain. We don't want to hear of its presence. We don't like remembering the agony of the past. We like the attractive, beautiful figures in our living room nativity scenes. We enjoy running our fingers over them as we listen to carols in the background. We don't want to be told what happened there, nor do we want to picture what it was like.

So we bake cookies. Decorate our homes. Plan parties. Give gifts. And from afar, respond to the needs of destitute people. We like candlelight, beautiful music, and sentimental stories. We enjoy all these things for they give us happiness.

But we also confess that the Christmas event has become more an escape than a resource. It speaks the language of garland and tinsel; we no longer think of it meeting the deep needs of our lives. We don't associate the transforming Bethlehem story with the problems of our time. If has become a happy time stripped of the depth of meaning from which it arose.

We don't want to be people who say, "Bah humbug!" to Christmas. But even more we don't want to lose the good news that pain is not our end, our punishment, or our cross. Rather our pain has meaning and if we have the faith of Joseph and Mary, it will lead us to a purposeful life we can now only scarcely imagine. What hope Christmas brings! What joy! In the name of our Master. Amen.

10 Is there, O God, a special person to whom we may give a gift this year? Someone, in addition to family members and friends, who is in need of an unexpected "I remember you." Help us to position our spiritual antenna to pick up that special person's name. May it be a person who is not in a position to do us a favor. Nor let us choose someone because we want him to know how wonderful we are. Let it happen in silence and without fanfare. Then our pleasure will be in the "no strings attached" element of the joy of gift giving. Once the gift is given, then may it drop from conscious thought — lest we be tempted to look for some kind of pay-back.

May this be the rebirth of Christmas in our hearts. Isn't this the way, our Redeemer, that you gave yourself to us in Jesus Christ? So in your name, we wish to extend your gift to another. In the spirit of Jesus Christ we pray. Amen.

Advent

11 Our heavenly Parent, you came to us as a helpless boy-child seeking to win our love and faithfulness. How different you are from earthly rulers, presidents, and kings.

We have wondered sometimes if you truly understood us, the men and women you created. Certainly you knew how enamored we were of ourselves. You saw how easily we robbed each other, and told lies about one another. We hardly qualified as those able to give your Son the care and compassion he needed to become our Lord and Savior. And yet you gave him to us anyway.

Your faith in us is staggering. How did you come by it? What is it you saw within us that prompted you to place in our hands your most precious child? We can scarcely think of it, your Son, in our hands.

Is it possible that we can see in ourselves what you see? That underneath the play acting and posturing there lives a soul capable of reaching out in tenderness and understanding. Help us to achieve this goal. In our failure to see beyond our own preservation, we kill each other. Our children, watching us, take weapons to school and, through a growing hardness of personality, learn to keep all others at a distance.

Grant us wisdom to understand what you have done for us. Grant us the courage to reach out toward others in compassion. Grant us the faith we need to rely always on you. Grant us the grace to see the wondrous love you have placed within our souls.

These words we pray in the name of Jesus Christ. Amen.

12 Our Sustainer, we depend on Christmas to bring us the happiness and laughter that we may experience in such short supply the rest of the year. Sometimes this scheme works. It may be a Christmas card from a long forgotten friend who reminds us of a more playful and carefree time. It may be the singing of a carol that lifts us from a routine mouthing of the words to a new spiritual insight about the nature of our Christ. Or it may be a family member's gift that reveals how thoughtful he is — loving us far beyond our deserving. Truly it is a time of happiness and hope.

But not all of us are rewarded in such beautiful and sensitive ways. Sometimes the days of Christmas pass by and we remain depressed and empty. We force a smile, but there is no counterpart of happiness in our hearts. We say, "Thank you," to our gift givers, while we wonder how they could give us something so far removed from our interests.

Later we return to work and school and gush to our friends, "Oh yes, the holidays were very good to me." We don't want to lie, but even more we don't want to admit that this holiday of holidays was such a disaster.

O God, turn our losses into gains. Enable us to see the promise and joy in these days, and then enable us to engrave these images into our hearts and memories. Much isn't always more. Shiny isn't always beautiful. Loud isn't always fun.

May we fine tune our spiritual sensitivity toward you, O Lord. We know that you often choose to make yourself known in silence. May we never let the celebration of these days sweep away the meaning of that first soul-stirring manger scene. Emmanuel! God with us. Amen.

13 Our Redeemer, 2000 years ago a series of unbelievable events took place that still stir our hearts and minds. A young woman became pregnant through the activity of the Holy Spirit. Her husband-to-be was told of this astonishing act and he believed what he was told. Because there was no room elsewhere, the young mother gave birth to her first-born in the stall of a cattle barn. Shepherds and wise men came and bowed down before this infant, for he was to become the Savior of all mankind.

Whatever explanations we have contrived to make these events plausible have often fallen short of the goal. Some people have decided that they were fanciful tales told by those in great need of being rescued from the emptiness and drudgery of their lives. But more of us believe this magical/mystical string of events did happen. We may have some doubts which we keep hidden, but mostly we believe. We believe because we have faith in you, our Father, who orchestrated these events. Certainly you are no stranger to miracles.

Through your Son — in whose honor we worship this day — you healed the diseased and disfigured. You provided orderly thought where insanity once ruled. You rescued people from despair and death.

We believe because we need to believe. We need a miracle to eradicate the darkness of our lives. We need more than a "there, there, now." We need the strength of faith to renew our brokenness of mind and body. The enormity of our evil is at last no match for your forgiveness and healing. How great is our need to believe. We pray through the compassion of the Holy Spirit. Amen.

14 Again, our Redeemer, we are shaken by the events of this world. Once more sons and daughters return home from foreign lands in caskets, drowning us in sorrow as we try to understand what is happening.

Are our young people dying for a noble cause? Will their pursuit of the enemy assure us freedom? Will their spilled blood give us hope for a better future? We dread the moment when we will hear the lonely sound of "taps" as another service person is laid to rest.

We don't weep alone. Tears flow in countries and continents all around the earth. Wives and husbands, brothers and sisters, parents and grandparents everywhere are asking the same question we ask — why do we persist in killing? Why must it be our loved ones that die? Why do we insist on dominating each other? Why do we continue to turn to guns — when it is clear that they have never achieved peace and joy? Even so, many of us feel vulnerable without guns.

Your Son came into our world as a defenseless baby. He was pure, guileless, and innocent. But we feel better served if we have a weapon within arm's reach. To practice the way of purity, guilelessness, and innocence seems to us to be folly in our hostile world.

As a nation we have decided to arm ourselves with weaponry that will deter attack from any outside force. As individuals we have followed the same scheme in protecting ourselves from our neighbors.

O God, we give ourselves to you not knowing how to stop our killing and in great need of your Son in our hearts. We confess that we are more ready to fight than to love or understand. Help us to see that obeying your Son leads us to the life we need, while guns lead us only to one more round of mayhem and death.

We pray in the name of the great Peacemaker. Amen.

Advent

15 Heavenly Parent, is it presumptuous of us to inquire how you felt when you sacrificed your Son for us? Besides your love — your unbelievable love — what else did you feel? There must have been pain and sorrow. Anguish. Loneliness. We don't really know what we'd do if you did tell us — except in some of our silly daydreams, we imagine what it would be like if we could repay you. Like children dreaming that, when they are grown up, they will give their parents the most lavish gifts the world has to offer. Then as they grow older and reality settles in, they recognize that these lavish gifts will never be theirs to give.

Reality has settled in for us as well. We know we can't repay you. In fact, we would be embarrassed if our friends discovered that we had even harbored such thoughts.

But then again we don't want to forget our dreams completely. We remember our children bringing us their crayon drawing, and how pleased we were to accept their gifts. How pleased they were that we took such delight in their handiwork.

May we bring our childish scrawls to you? These lives we have fashioned across the years — will you accept them? The truth we've learned, the beauty we've made, the service we have undertaken — may we lay them at your feet?

We sense that others might make fun of our gifts. We can even hear their voices, "Grow up! You're not a child anymore. Get real."

But it is also true that there is an irrepressible joy that mounts within us when we turn to you with our gifts in hand. Here, Lord, receive us. We are all that we have.

In the name of Jesus Christ we pray. Amen.

16 Eternal Spirit, as our eyes grow accustomed to the darkness and begin their search in the skies above Bethlehem, what is it we are to find beneath that fabled star?

We don't expect to find a Christmas tree, or thousands of twinkling lights, or an avalanche of beautifully wrapped gifts. Nor do we expect to find a simple solution to peace, or some quick reply to the problem of evil. We don't hold on to the false hope that once we view the manger, sorrow will never engulf us, and all struggle and pain will be taken from our lives.

Isn't there something more than the anxiety of a father for his crying, newborn son, or the exhaustion of the mother spent in childbirth? Surely this whole event isn't limited to the crudeness of the stable, the innkeeper's lack of sympathy, or even the adoration of the shepherds.

What brought those people to the stable that first night, is what brings us still. We hope, O God, to find you. We want to assure ourselves that your Spirit has made its home in our flesh and in our behavior. How beautiful are the words, "Our God and King!"

Our Light, open our eyes. Remove the blindness of doubt, fear, pride, and selfishness that our vision may not be impaired. Help us to see through the Christmas story back to the intention of your heart. Permit us to come to you, not only to confess our sin and the needs of our lives, but to offer ourselves in adoration.

May the wonder of your coming always be preserved in our hearts, we pray, in the name of your Son, our Lord and Christ. Amen.

Christmas Eve/Christmas Day

17 O God, was it cool the night Jesus was born? Did someone attend Mary other than Joseph? Or was he the midwife as well as the husband? Did Mary cry out? Did Joseph panic because he didn't know what to do? Were there women who came running to the stall, because they heard that a girl was giving birth to her first-born? Did they wipe the perspiration from her forehead? Did their words, "Everything is coming along just fine," reassure her? Did they bathe the baby Jesus and give him to Mary in swaddling clothes? Did they know he was the King?

Did Mary remember what the Holy Spirit had told her only months before? Could she affirm to herself that she was holding the Savior of all the world in her teenage arms?

Did she worry that the straw might get into his blankets? Did she fret because she wasn't sure when to nurse him? Was she concerned that the stable was such a crude shelter for God's Son? Or did she cast her worries aside, and for this hallowed moment, cradle her son, running her fingers across the soft curve of his cheek, and exult in the joy of giving birth?

Help us, Giver of Life, to remember that night, that young father, that young mother, and that defenseless, innocent child who was destined to be our King. Amen.

Christmas Eve/Christmas Day

18 In the scripture you instructed us, O God, to "be still, and know that I am God." Tonight is one of those still times. The frenzy of Christmas preparation is past. All that we can do for this celebration has been done. It will no longer serve any good purpose to push for the completion of two or three more tasks. So we become silent. Silence is often the traveling companion of awe. It envelopes us when we come face to face with a miracle. This is the moment of the Christ-child's birth.

Tonight is a time for hope. Hope for a good life, for peace, for love. If we can receive your Son into our lives this night, O God, isn't it possible that we can welcome him at others times of the year? If under his influence, we can reach out to meet the basic needs of our friends and neighbors at this time of year, then isn't it possible to carry out this ministry throughout the rest of the year?

This is a time for joy. How wonderfully, O God, have you cared for, nurtured, and loved us. We have broken our vows to you — our promise of faithfulness — yet when we turn to you in shame and confession you take us back. We know of no greater joy than your eternal, forgiving love.

Thank you for the unique and inclusive fellowship we enjoy with each other. We pray in the name of your Son born this night in far away Bethlehem many years ago. Amen.

Christmas Eve/Christmas Day

19 (A child's prayer)

God? We children didn't know if it was all right to pray at a Christmas Eve service, so we asked our pastor and he said he'd be glad to have us give a Christmas prayer.

First of all, God, we want you to know that we like all the lights and decorations and stuff. Our dads told us that some families have laid out a bundle to string lights on the outside of their houses. They think it's a waste of money. But dads often think that.

We think the Christmas story is cool. Mrs. Smith, our Sunday School teacher, told us that Mary and Joseph walked, well, Mary rode a donkey some of the way, and it took them over a week to go from where they lived in Nazareth to Bethlehem. Since there were no motels they had to sleep out at night. That would have been great! But our moms say, "Not if you're carrying a child!" Moms always bring that stuff up.

There's something that bugs us. Last year, at this one child's home, everyone opened their presents together, but Aunt Sylvia only got a couple of gifts from the children. So someone asked Uncle Leonard why he hadn't gotten Aunt Sylvia anything. He said, "She's already got everything — and she's too old for presents anyway." Is it true, God, can you get too old for presents? If it is, Aunt Sylvia doesn't like it, cause she began to cry and left the room. Uncle Leonard acted like nothing had happened. Some of the children in that family are going to get Aunt Sylvia a few extra gifts and sneak 'em to her when no one is watching. Is that all right? Sometimes old Uncle Leonard can be a pain.

We like it that you had your Son come to us as a baby. There's not much we can do to help adults, but we can do a lot for babies. Sometimes they cry too much, but other times they're great to look at and so warm and soft. Besides, they don't correct us, or tell us to go do something. It's okay with them if we rock them and talk to them. And since we'll never get to hold the real Jesus, would it be all right if we pretended with another baby? You know, like we had him here right in our arms and called him Jesus and everything?

We've already asked the adults and were surprised that our dads and moms and even grouchy Uncle Leonard thought it would be just fine. Sometimes they do come through. But they thought we should ask you first. So, God, what do you say?

We're the children from 12th Street and Wilbeth. And I guess we should say, "Amen."

20 Creator, we sometimes wonder about the small details of Jesus' birth. Perhaps we're foolish, but who assisted Mary in giving birth? We can't imagine it was Joseph, but then perhaps it was. If it was a midwife, who was she? Was Mary able to nurse Jesus immediately? How did Joseph and Mary find and prepare food for themselves? Did Joseph wash their blankets and clothing? Not likely. How long did they stay in the stable? When did Mary get back on her feet and begin to shoulder the responsibilities that were hers in their society? Did they choose to walk back to Nazareth to report that Jesus was born and everyone was doing fine? Or did they need to leave immediately for Egypt?

Pardon us for nitpicking at this beautiful account, but these are the matters that fill our days — that lay claim to our time and thought. These are the kinds of questions we ask to get a handle on what we think is reality.

That stable, what a primitive and barren scene it was. Compared to the level of care available to us, we look back at this setting and marvel that Jesus came into the world so healthy.

You decided, and then carried out your decision, to birth your Son in a very difficult and forbidding place. And you did this, not only for the salvation of Mary and Joseph's people, but for us as well. The story is overwhelming. Can kings and queens, presidents or chancellors, be given more than we? Can the wealthy be made more secure? Can the artist behold greater beauty? Can a counselor wish for a more life sustaining love?

We welcome you into our hearts, Lord. We shall follow in the footsteps of your Son. May the manger scene be so poised in our memories that it will be available to us at a second's notice. What love you've given us! In the name of our Master, we pray. Amen.

21 The stable in Bethlehem, O God, was likely no more crude or dirty than stables have ever been, but not as attractive as our bedrooms, and certainly not nearly as clean and resourceful as our hospital delivery rooms.

Yet within our imaginations — often inspired by an artist's brush — it is a warm, beautiful setting lighted by the grace and peace of the holy family. Underneath its splendor, there may well be the hard lines and shapes of reality, but our eyes can see only the glowing magnificence that radiates from that manger-crib. Crudeness is transformed into beauty. Rejection becomes acceptance. Fear turns to love.

So we stop in our rushing to look at a creche in a store window, and for a few seconds we wish with all our hearts that we could be a part of that idyllic scene. But then we come back to what we call our "senses," shake such a silly thought from our minds, and rejoin the hurried pace of our celebrations.

It is not possible for us to find a place for ourselves in that first century scene. But there is a place for the Christ-child in our twentieth century lives. Once he entered history the story of humankind was forever different. After we take him into our lives we begin a pilgrimage of renewal and hope.

So come, Lord Jesus, take your place in our hearts. We are in great need of you. Too easily we become the victims of hatred, lethargy, and fear. Until one day we make the awful discovery that there is no light within us — we are in darkness and unable to make our way. Come, Lord Jesus, with your touch, rekindle our flame. Light our path, make new our vision. We pray in the name of our Lord and Savior. Amen.

The New Year

22 A new year is just ahead, O Holy Spirit, and we wonder what it holds. It is surprising that we can shuck off the ugliness of the present year and look forward with hope to the next. It isn't that we have not been moved and shaped by dreams unfulfilled, and pummeled by stress from all directions. We are not deaf. We are not dumb, or stubborn. But we choose to believe in you through your Son and so the attitudes of defeat and cynicism are repugnant. Rather, equip us to stand boldly at your side.

Enable us to lay down the attitudes and practices that crush us, causing us to disengage from life in the hope we can save ourselves. Help us when we are frightened by life's events, to take strength from your nearness. Assist us to stand back on our feet when circumstances have trampled us. Remind us that love is the goal in all our endeavors, and help us not to settle for any imitation.

How grateful we are that you are God, and that you shared your Son with us, not only to come to know you more truly, but to reveal the winning and faithful life we can live. How precious your gift.

We pray in the name of our Lord and Savior. Amen.

23 Now, our Creator, we turn to a clean white page. We are very careful, for we don't want to blot or soil the first page of this new year. We want to begin neatly, without a blemish — at least on this first day.

Some of us are eager to welcome this new year, for last year was a very bad one. Others of us are reluctant to move ahead for this past year was very good. But time never slows or hurries its gait. It simply keeps moving.

We invite you, our Savior, to be our guide in the time allotted to us. May your complete trust in God, your Father, be our trust. May your care of us and others, be our care. May your faithfulness to truth, be our faithfulness. May the strength you gained from your Father, be our strength.

Today as we worship in this quiet, beautiful place, it seems that we can surely live a positive victorious life. But when we are engaged in the actual activities of daily living, then we become aware of how baffling and overwhelming life is. We are sorely tempted to march through our days with only ourselves in mind. To stop and decipher what is happening in our relationships — bringing us such a clutter of thoughts and emotions — is so burdensome.

However, Lord, we remember that when we stop to consider others, the eventual reward is the love and peace we long for. Forgive us our haste, our carelessness, and our selfishness. In turn we pledge to listen carefully to your instruction and to take joy in your Father's gift of time. We bring to you our present moment. Amen.

The New Year

24 One of the inescapable dimensions of our lives is time, a gift, our Creator, from you. In it we have the privilege of learning to know you and to enjoy your creation.

We are precisely measured by segments of time. On a given day we squall into life, on another we quietly cease breathing. We begin a task one day and finish it another. We are marked by beginnings and endings.

Time never varies its pace. Some days it seems to streak like a comet, yet in others it rides on the back of a turtle. It is claimed that on average we have 625,000 hours to live. At the beginning of life that seems like an eternity. At the end it isn't nearly enough.

We have numbered our days and years, Lord, so we can more clearly remember. We have even assigned a year marking the birth of your Son and another for his death. He fell far short of 625,000 hours. However, all he needed to do, he accomplished in the time given him.

So teach us to number our days that we might become wise. Enable us to learn from the past, but not attempt to relive it. Enable us to foresee what the future might be, but let us not waste time in daydreams. Enable us to be centered in the present, but not to make it the only time span of our lives.

We are grateful that our dismal failures of the past need not be a burden for today and tomorrow. May your forgiveness grant us freedom.

So today we act in new ways. Your Son has given us the key of confession, that, once turned, makes possible a new direction, a new life.

We are grateful for tomorrow. You have made it possible for us to choose health and wholeness in our todays, which in turn prompts them to reappear in our tomorrows.

Thank you for time. May we use it in faithfulness to you. We pray in the name of our Lord and Savior, Jesus Christ. Amen.

The New Year

25 We are an impatient people, Lord. We want what we want, today! If we have to wait, we begin to wonder if what we want is worth it. Perhaps something else can be substituted. Waiting for several more days is just too long. With the aid of modern technology we can make high quality realistic copies of ancient art, sculpture, furniture, and clothing. Instant antiques. We want instant justice, instant drug control, instant wealth, instant success. If we were in charge of nature we might move the brilliant colors of autumn right next to the new growth of spring, because we get tired of the cold, dark days of winter.

But for all our technical cleverness we've been unable to change the pace of time. It moves in its steady, unalterable way bringing us the tender shoot, the full green plant, and then the harvest.

Help us to remember that at the right time you brought forth your Son, born of woman, born under the law, that we might be adopted as your children. This you did not at just any point in time, but at the right time.

Teach us to appreciate time, to let it become our friend, to move in harmony with its rhythms. Enable us to stop railing at how fast it moves, or how slow. It was your wisdom that placed us in time and we would become wise to its ways.

These words we bring to you, our God, through the activity of the Holy Spirit. Amen.

Epiphany

Epiphany/Epiphany Season

Sundays After Epiphany

Transfiguration

26 We wonder, our heavenly Ruler, about the three wise men who brought gifts of frankincense and myrrh to the Christ child, some months or years after his birth. What a presence they must have made in Bethlehem. Did the commonplace appearance of the Holy Family's home cause them to think they might have come to the wrong place? Did they wonder about the plainness of the friends of Joseph, Mary, and Jesus? Perhaps they stepped outside their abode to recheck the position of the guiding star.

Did these humble friends quickly step aside to show proper respect for these men of high station, or were they so taken aback by their appearance that they remained frozen where they stood?

Were the wise men comfortable with the magnitude of their gifts, or were they embarrassed that their gifts overpowered the starkness of the people and the setting?

Were the shepherds and servants troubled that they did not give comparable gifts? Or did they take comfort in what they gave this young family at the crucial moment:
* a clean bed made from fresh, new straw
* the care of midwives
* a stable for bedding down their donkey
* assurance that everything would go well
* the words of the angels' new song?

We hope they sensed the importance of the moment and their place in it. We hope the wise men told these caring people how appreciative they were of their service. It's not too much to expect of men who had already sensed, through a dream, the real motive of Herod's supposed interest in worshiping the Christ Child.

Dare we intrude upon this scene? What gifts can we bring? Does it matter with whom we stand? Are we watching out of the corner of our eye to see what others may think of our gifts? Or do we trust that the gift we bring is the gift that brings joy to our God? That it is measured only by the love we have in our hearts for that infant child, in whose name we offer this prayer. Amen.

27 Sometimes, our God, we try to imagine what our world would be like if your Son had never come. And the wise men had never made their trek to Bethlehem. What if the empires of his day had continued on and on, without challenge from him or his disciples? What if the religious people of his land had become more and more entrenched within their restrictive laws? What if license had been mistaken for freedom? What if orgies had been mistaken for joy? What if the stealing and looting had been mistaken for victory or achievement? What if taking the spoils of war had been mistaken for ownership?

What would our world be like absent of the great architecture that marks so many of our churches and cathedrals? What would our museums be like if emptied of all the works that are directly or indirectly related to Christ and his church? And our music — who would be our composers if Christ and his bride, the church, had never graced the earth? What would we sing on the first day of the week? And literature, what would it say? What meaning could we extract from it? Would there be another Lord's prayer, or words for love as in 1 Corinthians 13? Would we have a concept of freedom? Would we believe in our own worth? Would we be empowered and motivated to strike out after some dream? Or would we be treated brutally, held captive, spit upon, and told we were lucky to draw our next breath?

The great goodness your Son brought to us is far greater than 1000 moral codes. His love for us is so staggering that we can scarcely take it in. His hope for our achievement — even unto perfection — leaves us inspired with hope and joy.

How can we thank you for the gift of your Son? Amen.

28 Our Savior, you reveal yourself in the most surprising ways. For example, we stepped outside the other day and grumbled about the newly fallen snow and how slippery it would be underfoot. Then for some reason we stopped, lifted our heads, and saw the splendor of the snow, blanketing the hedges, fence rows, and roofs. In those few seconds we witnessed your presence.

The other evening there was a face on our television screen of a young service man speaking from a foreign land. He was attempting, as best he could, to send his love, and to reassure his family that he was well. His words were halting and not well chosen, but our attention ignored his words and rested on his face that so eloquently expressed his concern. In those few seconds we witnessed your presence.

We stood in line at the grocery store, growing impatient because the cashier was taking time to listen to an older lady drone on about something we felt was unimportant. Then just before she took her grocery bag in her arms, she reached over and patted the cashier's hand and said, "Thank you." In those few seconds, we saw you reaching through the shroud of loneliness to arm a person's heart. And we witnessed your presence.

Where else may we see you, O God? Focus our vision so that we are enabled to see you in many other places and events. We are most grateful to meet you as often as we do. How reassuring it is to know that you are near, even when all demonstrable truth of your presence has flown away. In the name of Christ, we pray. Amen.

29 We thank you, God, for open doors.

It is our experience that what begins as a new and hopeful plan, within a few years becomes a rut, a stifling experience. Nothing seems to change. The people are the same. Our duties are the same. The landscape is the same. The music is the same. We might have stayed in this prison forever, except that you provided an open door. Your thoughtfulness and creativity caught our interest and off we went through that door to set foot on a highway we had never traveled before.

You asked to join us on the way and nothing has been the same since. We had lost hope and didn't know it. Now black and white have disappeared and color is here. Our values, worn smooth, had become dull and boring, but now we long to tell someone what an exciting place this world is. The hymns that we sang from rote are now bristling with meaning. Prayer that had become perfunctory is now the highlight of the day.

Others looking at us may not see how we have changed, but we are on the inside so we know that the old is past and the new has come. Thank you, God, for traveling beside us and taking us on roads we could never have imagined.

We praise your name and in your Son's name we offer this prayer. Amen.

30 Our Creator, we understand the role that winter plays in the growth cycle. Snow and ice, as treacherous as they are, have their place in our seasons. Dead stalks, crumbled brown leaves, and barren trees are not nature's enemy, but an integral part of its life. This is the knowledge we have gleaned from what we have been taught and from we have experienced. While we become impatient for the arrival of spring, we take comfort that it will come. We know from the past that our hope will not be disappointed.

But the presence of ice and snow, dead stalks, crumbled leaves, and barrenness in our personal lives is utterly devastating. We have been rejected, frozen out of others' lives. Sometimes we know why, but often we don't. We cry out that this can't be. Surely they don't mean to exclude us. If only we could sit down and talk, we could work it out. But they refuse. We see no hope in the ice and snow of our lives.

Nor do we see any good in death, poverty, sustained illness, natural catastrophes, hunger, or war. Yet all of these have been a part of life across history. We are angry and frightened that we are made to endure such trauma, especially when we — as we see it — have struggled for what we sincerely believed would make a better world.

This same anguish is to be found in the suffering and death of your Son. Why this perfect man had to endure the cross and death remains a mystery. Oh, we know the answers we give each other, but today we are talking about the gut-wrenching feelings that rise within us that exhaust the patience we have with truth. But we do know this, that on the heels of his pain and sorrow, he was resurrected from a death that was to hold him prisoner forever.

While we can't explain suffering, we know it to be; and while we can't explain life after death, we trust it to be. For this is your Word and our faith — so help us God!

Today we look outside searching for a sign of spring. We also look to you for the first signal of the coming story of resurrection. Enable us to hear, once again, that we will rise from the death within and about us. As your hope and love prevailed for your Son, so we pray, it will prevail for us. Amen.

31 Our Lord and Creator, we thank you for the gift of your Son, Jesus Christ. When your spoken and written word failed to win our hearts, you sent us your only Son that we might, at last, turn to you in faith. Knowing that we are unable to rid ourselves of our brokenness, you provided a way for us to obtain healing.

How glorious was that day when we confessed the destructive deeds of our lives, and you erased forever the nightmare of our sin. You granted us a new life, a new way, a new and certain hope. Not just once have we stumbled since then, but many times, and you have always been waiting for our return. Furthermore when we confessed our sin with a broken heart, you heard our confession and granted us a new heart. When we stood before you ashamed, you granted us dignity and poise. Even when we failed to honor your wondrous and amazing grace, upon our admission of failure, you willingly received us still. No words can express our gratitude.

We thank you, God, for hope that bursts upon us as sunshine cuts through the bleakness of an overcast sky.

We thank you for wisdom that enables us to see how all the fragments of life come together to make creation whole.

We thank you for faith that steadies us when we are being buffeted about by the cross currents of life.

We thank you for the love that overcomes all the fear and hostility that attempts to take control of our lives.

In the name of Jesus Christ we pray. Amen.

32 Eternal Spirit, sometimes it is nearly impossible to believe that you are interested in each one of us. If we were the president, or the vice-president of our country, a representative, a senator, a chairperson on the board of a huge company, the pope, a bishop, or an executive of a denomination — then likely you would make time for us. But you know and we know the vast majority of us are important only to a relatively small circle of friends and family. The media doesn't hunt us down to get our opinion on the latest social issue, or what we intend to do in the face of some international event. What we wear will not start a fashion trend. What we do won't make the headlines in the tabloids at the grocery checkout counter. According to our world we are the small people, unheralded and unknown.

Then we turn to the scriptures and learn that the image we have of ourselves is not the image you have of us. We are not small people. Through Christ you revealed that you had time for the oft-married woman who came to the well in the heat of the day. You gave attention to a common thief on the cross, a forgotten man at the pool of Bethsaida, a shrieking blind man, a hassled homemaker, an unknown sinner begging for mercy, a poor woman giving her last coin to the temple, a father who was desperate to have his child healed, and a crazy man living in a cemetery.

Your Son recruited a tax collector and a fisherman and transformed them into religious leaders. He raised a friend who had fallen into the sleep of death. He continued to love a disciple who denied him. He took time to provide for his mother's care as he hung dying on the cross.

Jesus never did seek out the important people; rather, he sought out everyday people. After bringing the Word to these people, he brought it to us.

O God, we don't know how you can possibly relate to each one of us. Because it seems an impossibility to us, we are tempted to think that it can't be true. So we are challenged to reach out to you in faith. And what a leap of faith that is! Now we know that you care for each of us — every last one of us. Is there a greater love? A greater miracle? How grateful we are that you are our God. Without you we would be lost and hopeless. With you we are victors in life and filled with unending joy.

O Christ, we pray in your name. Amen.

33 Sometimes, O God, we stand within our self-made world and believe that we are seeing all that can be seen. As we grow more accustomed to our world, we may even become convinced that our viewpoint of life is truth itself.

But when you come into our lives, our old world is broken into pieces and a new world rises from shattered remnants. What a fearful and glorious moment that is.

Save us, O God, from our so-called truths that imprison us. Bring us to your truth. Grant us the courage to see beyond truth as we have fashioned it, to the truth that is clearer than a mountain stream and more enduring than the mountains themselves.

Blind spiritual eyes present a challenge to become acquainted with life in new and different ways. A blind man leads to the death of our souls. He is forever at work keeping all aspects of life cornered into some kind of pinched understanding. Everything new becomes an enemy. Everything not understood gives rise to hell itself.

Holy Spirit, enter and dwell in our minds. May we know the joy that comes in a life ever renewed and everlasting. Thank you for your immeasurable love and grace. Thank you for open vistas, for sweeping, color-laden scenes, that leave us speechless in their grandeur. We thank you for your truth.

In the name of Jesus Christ, we pray. Amen.

34 We thank you, God our Sustainer, for the prayer ministry of our church. It is an honor to be given such a crucial and fulfilling task.

We are grateful that we can respond immediately to emergency needs through our prayer chain. We are grateful that we can come to you as a Christian family on Sunday mornings to respond to many different prayer requests. We are grateful that we can continue to pray individually for those requests throughout the week. You have given us such a significant opportunity for service.

How relieved we are when we learn that someone has come triumphantly through a life-threatening experience; or has been released from a body of agony, to come peacefully into your presence.

Most of the time, O God, we feel confident in our prayers, but there are those needs that confuse us. As a result we are not sure how to pray. On those occasions grant us the wisdom simply to hold the name of the people up to you, seeking your will for their lives. Enable us to be patient until we clearly understand how we are to pray.

There are those times, our Creator, when we are aware of the need, but feel no compassion for the people. Perhaps they have committed some heinous crime or indulged in some unspeakable immoral act, and as a consequence all we feel is revulsion. Lord, in such a moment is it still wisdom simply to bring their names to you — praying that your will be accomplished? Let us remove ourselves from negative prayer for fear that our anger or revulsion will only bring further damage.

We need to pray wisely, but above all we need to pray compassionately. May our love link with your love in reaching out to all manner of persons with all manner of needs. Our faith rests in the Apostle Paul's words, "Pray constantly."*

We bring these words to you through the life of our Master, Jesus Christ. Amen.

* 1 Thessalonians 5:17

35 When we were children, God, time passed so slowly. Especially when we were waiting for a birthday, Christmas, or summer vacation. Most of all we despaired of ever becoming an adult and making our own decisions. And even though it seemed exceedingly remote, we knew that someday our lives would end.

Now that we have become adults, heavenly Spirit, time moves quickly. With each succeeding year it moves ever swiftly. Now that we have the right to make our own decisions we are learning that we are still limited. Limited, if by nothing else than the ever decreasing amount of time still available to us.

So it is — as we experience time passing — we find ourselves becoming more interested in eternal life. Life with no end. What we know now is that life must be carefully rationed for each purpose, for we have only three score years and ten. But life everlasting will go on and on and on. Time, which has a beginning and an ending, will no longer contain us. How exhilarating! What a promise! Life everlasting is a dominating and overwhelming idea.

God, help us to live now as persons who will live eternally. May we shed the restrictions imposed upon us by time, that we may live in harmony with your coming gift of eternal life.

These words we offer you through Jesus Christ. Amen.

36 We are not always sure how to pray, Eternal Spirit. We don't know if we should explain how we see things, or describe the corrections we think need to be made, or point out that some persons should be made to apologize and others given praise. Likely you already know all these things; therefore there's no need to go over the same ground, a second or third time.

Then again, God, we want to make sure that you hear our story from us. We're greatly concerned for those we love, and those we fear. It's important to us that we speak directly to you.

Pardon us when we are testy, and hear us beneath our words, for we want to know your will and follow it. We cannot live fully in your world if we choose to be at cross purposes with your ways.

We do care deeply for the people for whom we pray, but that doesn't mean that we always know what to request on their behalf. It would be easier to ask for healing every time we pray, but sometimes healing isn't going to occur. We do die, so sometimes shouldn't we pray that our friends die peacefully — secure in your presence? And we often pray that pain be taken away, and yet it may be the needed factor to guide us or them back to health and wholeness.

Thank you, Holy Spirit, for being with us when we are unsettled and unsure. How good it is that we can come to you regardless of our circumstances.

Continue, O God, to teach us how to pray. Amen.

37 Sometimes, God, the problems confronting us seem insurmountable. Regardless where we search we find no resource or solution equal to the task. Then something we call "out of the blue" happens and brings our mountain to a molehill size and puts us in charge of our lives once more.

Sometimes, God, in the midst of confused and tangled thinking, our persistence for truth brings us an idea as bright and pure as simple wisdom. Immediately we know which path to choose. What a glorious moment!

Sometimes, our Savior, we think that the pain of our lives will surely destroy us. We are convinced we can no longer endure its tyranny. Then our faith in you brings us to a new door, and when we enter we come to a treasured place made available only to those who know pain. And we are grateful.

Sometimes, Eternal Spirit, we think that our sin is so deep, so pervasive, that no one's forgiveness will ever take it away. Then through a friend, a family member, or a complete stranger we come across a word, a phrase, a lyric, a line of poetry, a forgotten Bible verse that convinces us that the indelible mark of guilt can be erased after all. Then our hearts beat faster and hope takes up residence in our souls.

Sometimes, God, life brings us a shattering and devastating experience that only a week before we couldn't have imagined. Therefore we come to you as children in great need of your compassion and protection. We are grateful, O God, that you are our God. Who would we be, what could we become without you? In the name of Jesus Christ we pray. Amen.

38 One afternoon, dear God, we stood at the side of a road out west in what is often called "Big Sky Country." We were able to see the far distant horizons in all four directions. To the north a rain storm was in action, easily identified by its dark rolling clouds. To the east we could see hazy purple mountains stretching high into the sky, so high that we identified white clouds lower than the mountain tops, yet higher than the desert floor. To the south we enjoyed the brilliant sunshine highlighting green plants in between long stretches of sand. The west, behind us, was covered by gray-cast skies that seemed ominous and unrelenting.

The splendor of your world, Creator, attested by our eyes, nonetheless remained unbelievable. The grandeur of that place reached beyond what our minds could comprehend.

If your creation takes away our breath, then who are you? If we are unable to take into our beings the magnificence of our western lands, how will we ever look upon you? If our camera, paints and canvas, and memories fail to preserve the horizon's beauty in one moment of time, how will we grasp your eternal nature? As we struggle to know you in one place, at one time, you have already appeared in countless other places, free of any limitations imposed by place or time.

But you determined to bring yourself into our life, through your Son, our Lord and Master. He was one of us, who lived and died in our world. Limited to time and place, as we are, he gave us a way to come to you. What a sacrifice he and you made. You imprisoned yourself in our nature, providing us with a revelation of you that we could recognize and revere. How wondrous your love. How caring your Spirit. We thank you in the name of our Lord Jesus Christ. Amen.

39 O God, we bow before you this day in praise of your generosity. You have so amply provided for our needs. We, of all people on earth, are most fortunate to live in a land overflowing with every good thing. For many of us our homes are sturdy, our clothing is warm, our food is nourishing, and all these gifts come from you.

In addition, you have given us beauty to thrill our souls; friendship to warm our hearts; delightful experiences to make pleasant our memories; great stretching thoughts to challenge our minds; faith to steady our balance; insight and truth to reap a harvest from our most trying and distressing of circumstances. All these gifts come from your hands.

Even so, you have given us a greater gift. We have yearned, through all time, to become one with you, and to this end you have given yourself. As little children look to their parents to fulfill all their needs, so we turn to you. As little children seldom realize the true cost of the gift — the real extent of the sacrifice — so we little comprehend the enormity and majesty of the love that prompted the giving of yourself.

We bow to pay homage to you for a love that is far beyond our comprehension.

We ask you to help us understand you. We pray that the dividing walls of prejudice, pride, hatred, and fear be broken down so we can be set free to find our joy in you. Our everyday lives can become petty and narrow. Knowing nothing else we allow them to achieve the status of greatness. Then the day of monstrous need comes and we are caught by the smallness of our understanding. May the greatness of your love come flooding in, drowning all our pettiness, carrying us in to such service that causes your name to be further honored and your kingdom more excellently proclaimed.

In the name of the Lord Jesus Christ, we pray. Amen.

40 What, O God, should we make of Sunday? In the rush of days that often leave us breathless and unsettled, how is this day any different? Let's see, right after church there's lunch, then off to the mall. Susie's recital is at 4:30 and, oh yes, we almost forgot, we have guests coming over this evening.

And if you press us, God, we're going to defend our activities for what we are doing this afternoon and evening is "life enhancing." How about that?

We learn from the scriptures that this is a day of worship, a day of rest. We may know something about worship, but we're truly suspect when it comes to understanding rest. Rest is what we do when we jingle our keys, while looking at our watch, waiting anxiously for the next event to begin.

We can do something, always we can do something. It's resting that is difficult. We can do two things at once better than we can rest.

Unfortunately life brings us to some unwelcome rest periods, ready or not. We become ill and we have no choice but to rest. We grow older and have no choice but to rest. Life tumbles in on us and our fast pace only buries more deeply, than we have no choice but to rest.

We believe, O God, that you are serious, very serious — not just waxing poetic — when you say, "Be still and know that I am God."* Be still! If we don't learn what happens in the silence of your world, how will we make sense in the sounds of ours? As Christians we march to a different beat. An internal beat that is aligned with a very different rhythm than the dictates of our daily schedule.

Help us, Eternal Spirit, to go to that place within. Help us to be still. Teach us your silence.

We bring before you those persons who this day seek your will. Persons who hope for good health and comfort and who recognize that neither life nor death will ever carry them beyond the reach of your presence.

Let us be silent in the name of our Lord and Savior, Jesus Christ. Amen.

*Psalm 46:10

41 Your Son on the cross is a strange sight for the people of our day, heavenly Parent. Even we who believe have difficulty grasping all the significance of Jesus' heartless death. On one hand it seems preposterous that any man should endure this, but on the other hand, we admit that it attracts us, and compels us to come closer and closer until it captures us as no other event does.

Although we can't find words to explain Christ's obedience — especially to the cross — nonetheless, we sense he is right. Strange as it seems we are now convinced that he alone has secured peace and joy for us. What kind of man is he who would give up all that our culture claims as joy to possess finally the joy for which we all yearn?

Therefore, increase, O God, our understanding of your Son; but more than understanding, grant us the courage to follow the dictates of our hearts as we respond to his death. Empowered by that event we shall exchange good for evil.

This we pray in the name of Jesus Christ. Amen.

42 O God, our Creator, we thank you for our friends. How precious they are. They remember us on the special days of our lives. They speak well of us. They listen to our complaints, even when we repeat them. They tell us when they see something amiss in our lives. They love us enough to take risks on our behalf. Where would we be without friends?

Your Son instructs his listeners that he is their friend, "I do not call you servants any longer."* It was his desire to bring us into the citadel of his soul as his peer — on the very same level. What a marvelous turn of events. He prepares breakfast for us on the shore of the Sea of Galilee. He walks with us to Emmaus that we might have a clear and accurate understanding of his death and resurrection. He feeds us on the mountainside when we are without food. He calms the sea to give our boat safety and turns our fright into faith. How wondrous is our friendship with the carpenter from Nazareth. Accept, O God, our deepest gratitude.

We are mindful this morning of our friends who are ill and troubled. When we are plagued with poor health, or loaded with problems of home and work, it is easy to pull back and keep to a very narrow list of activities. Enable us to reach out to those who are going through wretched times. May we be the reminder that life isn't all negative — that the positive element is alive and well and living within their hearts. Today we remember our friends in prayer.

These words we offer through our Lord and Savior. Amen.

* John 15:15

43 It isn't easy, Good Shepherd, to see ourselves as we truly are. When we are at fault, we much prefer painting an innocent and blameless picture of ourselves, while attributing the ugliness of our lives to others. We defend and explain, defend and explain again, when we are identified as the one who failed. Then we attack and explain, attack and explain again that it is the behavior of others that is at fault.

But it isn't only our failure and wrong doing we hide from ourselves. We also keep from view our true strength, goodness, and effectiveness. We resist acknowledging the good things we do and are capable of doing throughout our lives. While we don't want to be seen as proud, still we need to own up to our gifts and abilities and make them available to you and others. This we need to accomplish so we can live in truth and know the happiness that you have set aside for us.

Our pride keeps us from seeing our failures, and our distorted self image keeps us from seeing our virtues and successes. In both instances we deny the truth. Forgive us. Grant us the courage to see our sin and the confidence to set free our gifts. We are wondrously created by your hand, our Creator.

This prayer is offered in the name of our Master. Amen.

44 Our Redeemer, how we need you. There's something unfinished within us that only you can complete. Something has gone wrong that you alone can make right. Something has become distorted and you alone can reestablish clarity. Something has become ugly and you alone can restore beauty.

We've tried, O God. We've spent ourselves pursuing solutions for our problems. We've read books, listened to tapes, attended seminars, prayed faithfully, worshiped thoughtfully, and we have come up empty. Why? Why should our effort be so sterile, so ineffective? We were so certain that we could take care of ourselves.

But you, gracious God, seek a broken and contrite heart. We've been fighting the day when we would come before you to confess our need. We have long hoped that we could make ourselves into something admirable and then present ourselves to you and you would say, "How good that you turned yourself around."

It isn't working out that way. We now know that we are powerless to overcome our brokenness and evil. So here we are. We present ourselves to you, no explanations, no excuses, no double-talk, no lies. We confess our false pride and our misleading and error-ridden knowledge. Secretly, we have always wanted to be you and now we own up to it and seek your pardon.

How grateful we are, how ecstatic, that you received us then and that you receive us now! You have presented yourself in our behalf to keep us from destruction and evil. What a price you have paid. How you love us.

Let the good news ring out. You make us whole. We are most thankful, our Savior. Amen.

45 When we were younger, O God, we could easily tell the difference between right and wrong. Or at least it seemed so. How many times we railed at the adult world, "It isn't fair," or "He cheated and you gave him the biggest piece anyway." We could spot injustice and cruelty a mile away, and we weren't fooled by a camouflage of adult words. Wrong was wrong and right was right.

Now we are adults and we no longer see things so clearly. Or is it that we can see the difference between right and wrong, but we don't want to acknowledge what we see?

Certainly our society has become more complicated. Having spotted some enemy, we turn to pick up our swords to lead the charge, but when we turn back, the enemy has changed or is nowhere to be seen. Sometimes our enemies turn out to be our friends. What's going on in our world? Can't we go back to a simpler time — back to a time when our forefathers told us the truth about life and it remained the truth?

Even if we don't understand the world around us and are frightened and saddened by the heinous behavior of our brothers and sisters, nevertheless enable us to stay connected to hope.

We do have hope. If traveling on one road leads to a dead end, then we shall find another. If we don't or can't understand the character of our society, then we shall find that portion we do understand and will give ourselves to its growth and continuance. If the negative, the destructive, the nay-sayers would crush our dreams of health and wholeness, then we shall turn to you, the author and finisher of our faith. You are God. Therefore, we have hope.

In the name of Jesus Christ, we pray. Amen.

46 O God, our Savior, we praise your name. With each new discovery of who you are and what you do, we learn all over again how magnificent you are. Our thoughts can't stretch far enough to encompass you. Our emotions, as wondrous and creative as they may be, cannot contain your majesty. For all that you have been, are, and will be, we praise your name.

Our Lord, we come to you in the act of confession. We've not been all that we can be. We can see beauty, but for reasons not always known to us we choose to look upon the ugly. We take delight in our neighbor's failure. We consort with evil, even when we know it is a dangerous ally. When we are able to speak words of understanding, we choose words that hurt and divide. Even when deep within we want to speak words of love, we turn to hatred and vindictiveness. Hear our confessions, God, and enable us to live within the pleasure of your love.

Our Creator, we come to you with burdens that rest heavily on us. We see the hungry and homeless of the world and we are pained, for we don't know how to make our resources available to them. We see the battered, the scorned, the poor and we turn our heads, for we don't know how to address problems that exist outside the realm of our experience. It brings to defeat our desire to help our neighbor attain joy and the good life.

Enable us to rely on you. In spite of the confusion and murkiness that permeates all facets of our lives, we choose to cling to you in faith. You are our hope for victory and triumph. You are our guide. Open the door that leads to the way we need follow. Teach us how to love and care for one another.

This prayer is offered in the name of our Master. Amen.

47 In honesty, Eternal God, we confess that we have doubts about a way of life — such as you revealed — that trades good for evil.

* We fear that doing good will encourage people to take advantage of us.

* We fear that doing good might jeopardize our chances of getting ahead.

* We fear that doing good will make us appear silly or naive.

But we also confess that living by the ways of the hateful — the loser's game — brings us distress. We are not happy with our hiddenness,

* stubborn arguments,
* ways of "getting even,"
* manipulation, and
* misshapen truth.

They only increase our distress, and drive us from love and friendship.

At last, after discovering that we are unable to free ourselves from our destructive ways, we turn, O God, to you. We know all too well the rejection, the hatred, the fear, the cruelty that exists in the world around us. Help us to play some part in healing these caustic wounds by offering:

* soft words for harsh,
* clarity for confusion,
* understanding for prejudice,
* hope for failure,
* kindness for insult,
* peace for hostility.

Let us turn to the way of the cross. In the name of Christ. Amen.

48 We are here this morning, O God, for our world has failed us again. We have followed the latest diet, purchased the latest fashion, memorized the latest "in" words, learned the latest dance step, and we're as lonely as ever. We felt certain that our new clothes, our new car, would change our image, but while our friends were happy for us, they related to us in the same old ways. We've read serious magazines, joined book clubs, taken evening courses, but we are as directionless as before. Our world leaves us empty, isolated. Sometimes we feel it rubs its hands in glee that we are so easily duped. Behind the masks of sincerity there is a lie. Behind the masks of honesty there is deceit. Then in the midst of it all, we shout out of desperation, "Our family will surely stay by us," only to learn that they have deserted us as well.

Lord, we turn to you for you are the same yesterday, today, and tomorrow. You have been faithful to your nation Israel. You have been faithful to your Son's bride, the church. And you were faithful to your Son. You have done what you said you would do. You keep your promises.

How good it is to turn to you this morning. Without our knowing it, we've been looking forward to this hour. The hymns lift our spirits. The scriptures grant us understanding. The prayers bring us healing.

We are thirsty and you give us drink. We are hungry and you feed us. We are rejected and you love us. We come to you for you are faithful. We praise your name over and over, Lord Jesus. Amen.

49 From the bleakness of our souls, O Lord, we turn to you. Our dark and empty mood leaves us frightened of the possible outcome of our days. We abhor the thought that we would become a shell, a front, a flat picture completely devoid of any depth or dimension.

Our emptiness isn't our desire. We have run and are running now in life's race hoping to win a coveted winner's wreath. It isn't that we have set our sights on hollowness, or that we wish to become shallow. Nonetheless, we find ourselves far from the spiritual home we dreamed of — lost and naked of spirit.

O God, we have tried to see our plight as the failure of our parents. We have accused them of failing in their love. Then in ever widening circles we have placed blame for our emptiness on our spouse, our family, our church, our schools, and our community.

But in honesty — for our polished exteriors don't deceive you — we confess that our predicament can be attributed to the roads we have taken, to the decisions we have made, to the foolish actions of our impulsive moments. To you we confess that we have already missed the mark.

We welcome your spirit into our emptiness that our lives may be filled. Then we will rejoice, for your strength is without limit, your love never leaves us lonely, and your ways promise fulfillment and joy.

In the name of our Lord and Savior we pray. Amen.

50 Gracious Provider, we are embarrassed to admit that we've failed to say "Thank You," for the many good things that have taken place in our lives recently. Even the little things, like finding the car keys (what a catastrophe that would have brought to our family's schedule), taking that first bite of cold, sweet, juicy grapefruit, and watching a sports event while enjoying the comfort of our easy chairs.

We are thankful for the good things that have taken place in the more serious areas of our lives, such as: receiving a note from a friend who reveals her sensitivity to a torn place in our lives, completing forms that give us an opportunity to choose the medical treatment we want at the time of our dying, and watching the slow arrival of spring knowing that it is not only the way of nature — but a symbol of what has been provided for our souls as well.

We thank you for the good things that have happened even in the holocausts of our days. After hearing that our time is limited, we find strength to endure through our loved ones. Failing at some critical point in our work, we discover a poise, a strength deep within that enables us to meet the crisis. Then, after experiencing the worst event we could have ever imagined, to find what power and peace there is in prayer.

God, it is so easy to be careless, but we do want you to hear us as we say, "Thank you," this day. We can not imagine living without you. Your love is the force that sustains us and we choose never to take you for granted. In the name of Jesus Christ we pray. Amen.

51 It must have been a dazzling moment for Jesus' inner circle to see the Master caught up in the company of Elijah and Moses there on the mountain top. The light surrounding these three blinded the disciples' eyes, and while the voice from heaven was reassuring, it was also terrifying. Their minds were unable to comprehend it. How could they adequately respond to this moment, that stole their breath away?

We understand Peter. He wanted to do something to memorialize the moment. So he offered the first thing that came to his mind — the construction of three altars. Not knowing what else to do, we have built churches, erected statuary, endowed seminaries, and placed thousands of brass plates on walls, pews, and stained glass windows. Surely there is something we can do to achieve a proper response to this man who takes away our sin.

However, your Son, O Lord, counseled his closest friends to say nothing of what they saw. Nothing. Rather they went down the mountainside and returned to their ministry of teaching and healing.

We are a people who build things, collect things, invest in things, determine our worth through things, and trust that the good life is measured in things. It is a surprise that Jesus squelched the idea of erecting altars. Rather he chose silence as the proper response to this event. When, at last, they broke the silence it was to proclaim the good news.

We, too, will tell of our Master's wonder and grace, but we will do this most eloquently in meeting our neighbor's need. Let our actions speak of your love and eagerness to redeem, O God. Let us not be so calculating in our caring. Let us shout through our actions the joy of our faith. Let us risk the use of our hands and feet, we pray in the name of our Master. Amen.

Transfiguration

52 We thank you, O God our Creator, for being so attentive to our world and to us. Your Son revealed that not one sparrow falls to earth without your knowledge, nor is there one hair on our heads that you have not counted.

These are staggering claims. Because we can't fathom how they can be true, we are tempted to consider them as exaggerations that speak more of daydreams than reality.

Yet it is true that you were there for us this past week. You were there when our weariness nearly caused us to collapse, and you enabled us to finish the day. You were there caring for us in a baby's winsome smile, in a friend's welcome compliment, and in a family member's "pitching in" to help us complete our chores. You were there telling us that we needed to listen and not talk. Again, you were there when we needed to step boldly forward and not back down. You were there when a loved one left this earth to be with you.

We praise your name for it is hallowed. We praise your wisdom for it is unfailingly true. We praise your patience, for you continue to wait for us even when you know that we aren't looking for you. Your greatness stretches our thoughts beyond our most imaginative words.

We offer ourselves to you, including what we know and what we don't know of ourselves. For you want all that we are, that we may become obedient. It is in our obedience that we come to know you more perfectly.

We pray in the name of our Lord and Savior. Amen.

Lenten Season/Easter

Ash Wednesday

Sundays In Lent

Community Lenten Services

Palm/Passion Sunday

Holy Thursday/Good Friday

Easter Sunday

53 Gracious God, how grateful we are that you are available to us. We find you in our Bibles and in the hymns we sing. We see you in nature — the largest mural ever created. We meet you in our friends and our brothers and sisters in Christ. We can reach out to you anytime, day or night, by simply giving attention to your Spirit within us. Who else is so available?

Yet we must confess that at times we don't see you. We can't find you. You are no longer near us. Then soon we learn that you aren't hidden. We are. Like Adam and Eve, we've done something that shames us and rather than face up to our wrongdoing, we decide to stay far from the reach of your voice. If we can't block out your voice we invite in other voices and sometimes add our own to the din. We become anxious when there is silence. We are afraid, for we realize we are vulnerable.

At last, we muster our courage and come to you in silence to confess our sin. How we decided to do what we did, to say what we said, isn't clear to us. That we are capable of such fear, hostility, stubbornness, and cold-heartedness alarms us. We thought all along that such feelings resided only in others.

The time for the charade is past. We come to you as we are, seeking your forgiveness. We want our wickedness to be transformed into courage and hope, that we might start a new journey for the rest of our lives.

How good you are to forgive. How beautiful life is again. Nature's splendor brings tears to our eyes. Our friends, we now discover, have been supporting us all along the way. How majestic and magnificent we find you in our Bibles and hymns. How near you are to catch us when we fall. May your name be praised forever. Amen.

Ash Wednesday

54 O God, we thank you for the promise of springtime; for infant birds breaking out of their shells; for flowers bursting out of the cold winter's earth. We thank you for children who say what we are too embarrassed to say; for friends who take seriously our private dreams; and for those who help us escape from our secrecy and loneliness.

If your Spirit is freedom, O God, then we see you in many places.

However, on this day, our worship reminds us not only of your works, but of our own. We are here to look inward, to prepare ourselves, to be in readiness for the death and resurrection of Jesus Christ. Looking honestly into ourselves is hard work. It is so much easier to delay, or to point out our neighbor's faults, for we are busy and our neighbor's faults seem so obvious. We are tempted to pray, "Dear God, help us find rest, for we are so harassed, and please take care of the insensitive man next door, he is making such a mess of things."

But we know in our sleepless nights that our prayers are not for the insensitive man next door, but for ourselves. We are the ones who can not see. We speak harshly and vindictively and can not see where the anger comes from. We keep pulling back from people and can not see nor understand our fear. It is so hard, our Father, to see how we contribute to our own unhappiness. It is as if we choose to hide from ourselves.

Therefore, we invite you into our lives to enable us to see what we are unable to see, or choose not to see, and thereby gain freedom from the patterns that would destroy us. We openly confess our great need for you.

In the name of Jesus Christ we pray. Amen.

55 It is not easy, heavenly Spirit, owning up to our mistakes — honestly presenting ourselves to you with all our imperfections. We choose rather to soften our confessions, offering them with "adjusted" explanations so they won't sound so dreadful.

We want you to believe that our sins aren't as bad as when they are committed by someone else. For that matter we want you to know, Lord, if others hadn't egged us on we wouldn't have erred at all! Grant us mercy, God, for we actually believe this. Help us to see our sin plainly and to talk to you openly.

It takes great courage and honesty to state the truth about our motivations. So we present our reasons for what we did, trying to assure you that we had only the best of intentions. But then when we are challenged, as Jesus challenged mankind centuries ago, we splutter as we attempt to cover up who we really are and what we are actually scheming.

Help us, O God, to walk a straight line. Let our "no" be "no" and our "yes" be "yes." May we take strength from our faith in you that we might also talk a straight line.

Enable us to honor what we can do. May we not despise the work of our hands and the product of our minds. May we treasure your gifts implanted within us and gratefully shape them to your purpose. Thank you for the possibilities of accomplishment and joy.

In the name of Jesus Christ, we pray. Amen.

56 You know our hearts, gracious God, how they carry guilt from the past. We've often yearned to go back in time just long enough to correct what we did wrong. Just long enough to wipe away the hurt and disappointment we caused our loved ones. Just long enough to erase the shame we feel.

You also know, O Lord, that some of us carry guilt unwittingly and we don't know why. We just feel guilty. We've tried to attach it to past events, but nothing explains it. Nothing warrants it. All we know is that deep within — beyond our reach to erase it but close enough that we can't forget it — is our elusive, persistent sense of guilt.

You also know, Lord, that we have guilt from recent days and we do know why. We know exactly what we did, but we keep hoping that it will go away and that those involved will soon forget. So we've blustered and denied any wrong doing. We've refused to talk about it. We've even tried putting the blame on someone else. But in our heart of hearts we know that we are wrong. Waiting until it blows over isn't going to work.

Help us, merciful One, to know the freedom that comes with the erasure of guilt — to know the joy of an unburdened heart.

If we need to go to those we've hurt to ask forgiveness, grant us the strength to undertake this embarrassing task.

How do we right the wrongs of the past? How do we become free of guilt that lurks always just beyond conscious thought, unexplained and persistent? If we can right some wrong, how grateful we would be to do that, for we are weary and defeated.

Enable us to trust completely and fully your words and acts of forgiveness:

"Forgive them, Father, for they do not know what they are doing."

"As far as the east is from the west, so far he removes our transgressions from us."

"If we confess our sins, he who is faithful and just will forgive us our sins."*

How many times do we need to hear these words? Until the time comes when they are written on our hearts, until we are no longer badgered by the continual din of our wrongdoing.

God, we do believe. Help us in our unbelief.

Thank you for a forgiveness that can reach further than we can go astray.

In the name of Christ, we pray. Amen.

* The above scriptures are taken from Luke 23:34, Psalm 103:12, and 1 John 1:9.

57 You, Holiest One, see us for the sinners we are, yet love us still. How will we ever find words to express our gratefulness? We love to build castles, God, but often in disrespect of you. Castles of self-pride that may be in our homes, our prestige, our power, our goodness. It pleases us to have others notice what we have built in our lives, and therefore it becomes necessary to devote all our attention to ourselves and to the things we do.

But this path eventually comes to an end. Somewhere along the line, self-pride runs out. Our path falls short of real happiness, or takes us on a by-path that is filled with the thistles of disappointment or the rocks of despair. However, your path isn't easily followed. It leads into treacherous areas also. The great difference when traveling your path, is the warmth and comfort of your hand and the knowledge that despite whatever happens, ultimately all will be well.

Forgive us our castles built in self love and in disrespect of you. Teach us that in the beauty of submission we will find the castle that will endure not only for the length of our days, but forever.

Watch this day over our church. Take unto yourself, we pray, the deep needs and the silent wishes of your flock. We beseech you to send healing and wholeness to replace disease and brokenness.

Accept our dedication to your will and keep us worthy of sharing life eternally with you. We pray in the spirit of our Lord and Savior, Jesus Christ. Amen.

58 Sometimes, O God our Creator, we seem so inadequate and so ineffective. How can we be considered your children? We look into all the corners of our being and we can't find anything worthy of your name. We'd just as soon pretend you don't exist than to marshal the nerve necessary to knock on your door. We've failed. What we have done dishonors you and what we haven't done blackens your name.

How can you love us at these times? Do you see beyond our lies, our petulance, our apathy? Do you see something in us we don't see — like courage, love, and faithfulness? Clearly you are on a different wave length, for while we wallow in despair and hopelessness, you are talking of the joy and triumph you see possible in our souls.

So now we pray that we see ourselves as you see us. We choose to fasten our vision on who you are and who you see within us. We confess our sin and ask that it be taken from us, as far as the east is from the west. We claim your promise of hope and joy and will begin living at this very moment as you have been living in our lives all along.

Hold us close in your love. When we can think no more, when we can pray no more, when we can express our faith no more — hold us in your love. We cannot manufacture the faith we need; you are the source that fills our emptiness. We can do no better than to come into your outstretched arms.

This we pray in the name of our Master. Amen.

59 O Creator, it isn't easy going back twenty centuries to a small desert-like province of the Roman Empire on the far eastern end of the Mediterranean Sea. It is a hundred times more difficult to believe that what happened there has any direct bearing on who we are today.

Yet if it weren't for the man Jesus, your Son, the Christ, would we even make the effort to know the Jewish people of first century Israel? Likely not. If Jesus hadn't been there, then Paul and Peter wouldn't have emerged as leaders of a transforming faith. As a consequence we would have turned this piece of history aside.

However, your Son Jesus lived then. He was there. As far as we know he never left his homeland, after his parents brought him back from Egypt. He didn't even travel extensively within his homeland. He taught, healed, forgave, and prophesied. He revealed himself to be a loving and wise man and, better yet, a redeemer who was able to rid his people of their sin.

It bothers us, Lord, that the leaders of his day didn't recognize that he was the long-awaited Messiah, your chosen one. It rankles us that his own disciples fled in terror when his life was on the line before the high priest and the Roman soldiers.

However, it is a source of hope for us, that not everyone gave way to anger or fear. There existed here and there those who had some deep inner resource. There were other people, much like us, who dreamed and hoped, but then turned bitter and gave up. They pledged their lives and drew their swords, but when challenged denied knowing Jesus and ran and hid. Then, at last, at the crucial moment, they relied on your Spirit and became people of unmatched faithfulness and courage.

In the Lenten season ahead, may we succeed in making the first century relevant to today's needs and hopes. Thank you, God, for everyday people.

We lift up these thoughts to you through the name of Jesus Christ. Amen.

60 O God, our Parent, you who care for each of us as if we were your only child, and who cares for us more than we care for ourselves, hear our words of praise. Our hearts find so much more to say than our words can express — even when our thoughts, though lofty and probing in character, at last can bring us only to the very edge of your ways. Yet to your sanctuary we come gratefully and expectantly, for while we are unable to find you through word and thought, you are always able to find us.

Discover us this day, O God. Come through all the density of our broken and tangled ways, along the pathways paved with promises and deep resolves and now grown over by weeds and bramble. Reach out to us, because we may fail to reach out to you. May someone worshiping here today feel you coming into his heart and upon leaving this place proclaim, "My God and King!"

Come to us, O Lord, in the spirit of dedication. For we are never helpful when all wrapped up within ourselves; never joyful when we are self-centered; never content as long as our purpose for living fails to reach beyond the accomplishments of our lives. Therefore, may we see, through you, some service we can render, some task we can perform, some soul we can assist.

Come to us in inner power. We seek not the easy course, the gold paved street, nor the soft and undemanding life. We do not request that we be spared the storms and hurricanes of life, but we pray for houses built upon rock that will not wash away with storms and strong currents, and will not crumble under the threat of destruction. God, discover us with your power that we may be strong within.

We pray in the name of our Master. Amen.

61 O God, you taught us through your Son that unless we become as little children, we will not gain entrance into the Kingdom of Heaven. Teach us how to be children again.

Children have a simple, direct, and unquestioning faith. Many of us, who pride ourselves on having some understanding of life, have lost that childlike faith. We are doubtful, questioning, and suspicious. We have been hurt and trampled when attempting to live this simple faith; therefore, we have pulled back, making sure never to be so vulnerable again. Oh, we still smile warmly, shake hands convincingly, pass along greetings cheerfully, but underneath this outward display we have already retreated from you and all our brothers and sisters.

We are not happy with whom we have become. We pray, O God, for the courage to open our hearts once more to our brothers and sisters and to you.

We seek a strength that will enable us to meet head-on the heartaches and confusions of our lives, not blind to the consequences, but confident that only in this kind of daring is the Kingdom of Heaven brought into our lives.

Many times, O Lord, we have seen children forsake their toys or friends to run into the arms of a favored loved one. They give themselves exclusively, totally. Our loyalties are divided, our interests are legion, our lives are jostled this way and that by opposing forces. (We can't give ourselves to our work because of the pressures of home, or we can't give ourselves to our families because of the pressures of work.)

It seems that your call to us grows fainter. We want you, God, to line up with all the other demands in our lives, and take what share might be yours and please don't pester us for more.

But, in truth, how we long to run to you, to throw ourselves into your care, to feel the strength of your arms, to know the warmth of your presence. How do we set aside all that blocks us from you? That's the question that haunts us. Teach us to be children again.

Encourage the love and understanding of the friends and members of this parish, we pray in the name of our Lord Jesus Christ. Amen.

62 O God, our Creator and Redeemer, we enter your presence humbly and gratefully.

Your mercy surrounds and protects us as a mother hen her chicks.

Your love is as endless as the grains of sand upon a beach.

Your justice is as sure as the coming and going of the seasons.

Your truth is as unshakable as the greatest mountain and as certain as the movement of the sun.

For all these images we give you thanks.

As your children we understand that these qualities of your character are to reveal themselves in our lives. But often, we confess, we are like the tumbleweed that moves this way and that with every gust of the wind. Under pressure we yield to the course that offers the least resistance, regardless of the consequence. In difficulty we cling to an ideology of anxious despair, as if all hope and reason had vanished from the face of the earth. We are weak, unsteady, sinful, and beg to be forgiven for forsaking your image planted within each of us.

Grant us quiet times, O God, wherein we can commune with you. Times when we can set aside the cowardice that binds us and welcome the strength and bravery of your will. Times when we can be free of all the entanglements of outer life, to feed our inner lives in intimate conversation with you. Times when we can claim the freedom you offer.

Now help us to keep foremost in our minds that we have a purpose for living. May we attach ourselves to the great ideas you have so wondrously provided. Spare us from the tedium of aimlessness — lest we wander from one event to another hoping we are in pursuit of truth.

Bless, this hour, your children assembled here. Meet the needs of their sorrow; lift the load of their burden; and shed your light upon their paths. May they trust the joy that wells up within them because you are present in their lives.

These words we offer in the name of our Lord Jesus Christ. Amen.

63 O God, our Creator, nearly every evening we see the aftermath of violence on our television news. Often it doesn't touch our hearts for we have become hardened to it. We see, but we don't see. Then we learn that two families are wiped out by two fathers who couldn't, apparently, contend with the conflict within themselves and their families. The pain and horror of their deeds seize us. Once the tent flap of reality is up, then comes streaming into our minds the violence triggered by racism, neighborhood gangs, hidden fury, irrational fear, and calculated shootings. The enormity of it causes us to push ourselves back in our chairs, as if that would remove us from our heinous world.

What can we do? Will the prayers of one congregation living in _____ (*name of your community*) actually make a difference? Will our Bible reading and church attendance subtly tip the scales from evil to righteousness?

How can you say, "Yes," to these questions so quickly, Lord? Do you say, "Yes," because you know that your Son, who died in a small eastern village of the Roman Empire, would eventually be able to redirect the course of the whole world? At the time only few people could see any good coming from his death and resurrection. But what a difference those few people made. While the difference didn't come quickly, it came.

We tell each other that all violence happens somewhere else. But we know in our hearts, it happens where we live.

We can be faithful where we are. We can be faithful at home, at work, in our community. We can honor the name of Jesus and speak of our love for him. We can give shape to our days from what he teaches and from who he is. We know that we can bring our hostility to Jesus Christ and ask that its energy be redirected into life affirming ways of living. Our lives can be redirected and they, in turn, can shape the world in which we live. Teach us not to belittle or scorn the living of our days. Rather, enable us to be obedient to your will for the transformation of our time.

Hear our prayer, O heavenly Spirit. Amen.

64 We suppose, our Creator, it is a great joy to be on stage and receive a standing ovation from hundreds, even thousands, of people. What joy to be given a coveted medal on some state occasion by the president of our country. But what are the expected joys in our lives?

One of them, we are convinced, is a baby's smile in response to our antics. We can block out everything and everyone about us to see if we can elicit that beautiful, innocent smile. As you know, Father, we can offer all kinds of silly behavior, strange sounds, and funny faces just to get the reward of one of those smiles. Even though the smile may last but a few seconds, we feel it was worth all the effort we put into our absurd little act. Flushed with victory we tell our friends, "There's nothing more beautiful than a baby's smile."

God, what would we be willing to do to gain your smile? We suppose that the silly things we do spontaneously and gladly for a baby are not in order. But what can we do? We have learned from the scriptures and the teachings of our faith that we can bring ourselves to you daily, offering ourselves to your service, studying and learning what your will is for us. Then we can reach that point where we are not distracted by others as we pursue our relationship with you, wherever it leads. In short, giving ourselves to you whole heartedly.

Peter was ecstatic when he saw Jesus, in his glory, talking with Moses and Elijah on the mountain top. Is it possible that we can see Christ in his glory, smiling on us in response to our efforts at love and prompting a joy that we can scarcely imagine?

In hope of the Master's smile we offer this prayer. Amen.

65 O God, our Redeemer, in the silence of this hallowed place, we come to you filled with all the cacophony of our lives. Our thoughts are tumbling on one another, pushing us first this way and then that way. Even when silence fills the space about us, we can still be distracted by all that is happening within us. We don't always know how noisy our inner lives are until we come to a quiet place.

Quiet can be unnerving. So we turn on the television even when we don't plan to watch it. "It keeps us company," we tell our friends. It also ends the silence. We turn the ignition key to our car, squeeze the handle of our drill, push the button on our microwave oven, set the dial on our washer, pull the rope on our mower, talk to the cat, the dog — even the fish, fold and unfold the newspaper, dial the telephone — anything but silence, anything.

What is so fearful about silence? Will something come to mind that we don't want to think about? Is it loneliness we dread? Or is it emptiness that gives us chills? Perhaps it is simply that we haven't given quietness an opportunity to be a friend.

Quietness isn't our enemy. It is where you dwell, Savior, waiting for the time when your word can be spoken, when healing can begin, when forgiveness can be granted, when joy can give shape to the rest of our days. So we enter into silence waiting and listening.

In quietness you will renew our spirit. Amen.

66 Across the years, Eternal God, there have been many things we desperately wanted. We remember when we were young wanting a stack of chocolate bars, a new pair of jeans, a recording of our favorite singer, a driver's license, a car ... We could so vividly imagine how wonderful life would be once we had what we wanted.

Now we remember that we lost interest in some of those items before we ever owned them. Or once possessing them we discovered that they weren't as wonderful as we first imagined. The disappointment left a bitter taste in our mouth.

Only later, God, did we learn that those yearnings were practice runs for our hungering and thirsting after you. You are our ultimate longing. It is you we desperately want and need. Even so, we often continue to imagine how wonderful it would be if we had this or that. Then life would become full and rich, and joy would surely be ours. Even with these treasures in hand, our joy is still destined to run out and then we will need to start searching for something else.

Now our attention is fixed on you. You satisfy our hunger. You slake our thirst. We need look no further. We are so grateful that we stopped our anxious searching. How good it is to live within the circle of your unending fulfillment.

It is one of the great pleasures of life, that we can speak to you anytime, day or night. You are always within range of our thoughts. With you there is no "call waiting." How you honor us with your presence. In the name of Jesus Christ we pray. Amen.

67 How beautiful and moving, gracious God, are your ways. "As far as the east is from the west so far you remove our transgressions from us." You renew our youth and crown us with a steadfast love that lives from everlasting to everlasting.*

No one has ever spoken to us as you have. No one else knows how to probe to the very depth of our soul and leave a message of faith, hope, and love.

Sometimes, when our days go well, we think ourselves to be capable and good. So we may be. Then when things go awry, we quickly discover how limited we are, and discover how resourceful you are. Your wisdom leads us to new solutions and higher vistas where we are enabled to see the truth as never imagined. How grateful we are.

Today we are especially mindful of our friends and loved ones who are in need of our prayers:

For those clinging to the last hours of life, we pray for peace and a beautiful passage home.

For those in pain, we seek relief. May healing come to refresh their spirits.

For those confused by the circumstance of their living, we request wisdom and patience.

For those who sorrow, we seek your comfort. Hold close our friends who have so recently come to know the chasm death creates.

For all of us who choose to walk in your ways, grant us insight and faithfulness. Guard us against ever failing to honor your name.

In the name of the Lord Jesus Christ we pray. Amen.

* Psalm 103:4, 5, 12

68 O God, our Creator, how blessed we are that you breathed yourself into us, making us in your image. What higher honor could we be granted? You have placed us over all creation — even above the majestic mountains and the rolling seas. No one can bring us a higher honor, or give us a greater commission.

Yet, Lord, we often ignore who we are and act in embarrassing and destructive ways. We walk through life as if we were defeated. We transact our business in an apologetic manner, as if we weren't deserving of a high quality of service. We forget that we are meant to make a contribution to life; rather we wait in some hidden place, hoping no one will see us.

Today, enable us to become the persons you wish us to be. Grant us the courage and wisdom needed to bring our work into victorious and productive days.

You alone can save us. We alone can say, "Yes," to your magnificent plan. In the power of the Holy Spirit we pray. Amen.

69 O God, sometimes your creation displays itself to us in such beauty and promise we are literally dumb-struck. Now, with the very first signs of life appearing in our lawns and gardens, we are held speechless by the promise of tomorrow's richness. Each day we keep searching for new evidence of your provision. Though we have seen nature's cycle many times before, in some indescribable way it is wondrous and new, all over again.

Not only do our lawns and gardens get a fresh start, so do we. It is our time of renewal. In these Lenten Sundays we will experience the passion of our Lord Jesus Christ as if we had never experienced it before. From a love too marvelous to describe, we are lifted out of our sorrow and defeat to live in hope and confidence. Who are we that you regard us so highly? What is the measure of our talents that you plan for us such certain victory?

We bring to your attention our family members and friends. How precious is each one. Accept our concerns, our hopes for those we cherish. Grant them what they need for the living of their days. We take joy in the certainty of your love.

Through our Lord and Savior, Jesus Christ, we pray. Amen.

70 Sometimes, God, in our desire to know you and to live by your truth, we become fixed into one particular way of worshiping, praying, and thinking. Then we lose our ability to adapt to the changes about us. Our faith, instead of being a lively resource, becomes an albatross about our necks. No longer do we search for new, inventive ways to respond to a challenge; we simply ignore the challenge.

We know this isn't the way of life brought to us by your Son. He invited us to embrace all of life; in fact, he wanted for us life abundant. So we pray this morning for bravery. Bravery to put cherished ideas to the test in the confidence that the repayment will be much greater than the investment. We pray for bravery that will enable us to step forward in faith.

Forgive us our cowardice. In the face of challenges we have run for cover. In the face of confusion and chaos we have thrown up our hands. In the face of an enemy we have meekly surrendered. Forgive us. In our confession and in our resolve to fight the good fight, may we turn to you as the resource we need to overcome whatever blocks our path. Thank you for being our light — the one who shows the way.

We offer our hearts to you through the Holy Spirit. Amen.

71 We come before you, our heavenly King, grateful for the faith you've given us through your Son, Jesus Christ. We confess that sometimes we take it for granted. But when something happens in our lives that causes us to turn to our faith, how thankful we are that it is there.

When we see people floundering, trying desperately to put their lives together, unable to turn to their faith because they have none, our heart aches for them. We wonder how we can share our faith without being "preachy" or tongue-tied. Help us to rely on you. Encourage us to speak of our faith as best we can, and to trust that you can use our words for your purposes.

We are thankful that we can bring to you the needs of our family members and friends. We hold them up to you. May your comfort come to those who sorrow, wiping away their tears. May your peace fill the lives of those torn apart by the conflicts within their lives. May your wisdom guide those who need to choose carefully the way they need to go. May your peace blanket those whose pain controls their day, as an unwanted tyrant. Above all, may your love find its way into our hearts, that our spirits may soar in the confidence that whatever takes place we will ever be by your side.

In the name of Jesus Christ, we pray. Amen.

72 O God, our Lord, you whose strength is unending, be with us when we falter in our faith.

As a little child, who has been instructed to stay clean, but has fallen and dirtied his hands and now comes running in tears to his parent, so we who know the better way have fallen. Unable to cleanse ourselves, we come imploring you to wash us so that we may become as white as snow.

We greatly need the strength of your wisdom. We need to see life and death from the perspective of eternity. We need to view our relationships from the ways of sensitivity and love. We need to view the use of our talents from the faithfulness implied in our commitment to you. Our understanding and wisdom need to be enlightened and instructed by your own.

We so greatly need the strength of your forgiveness. We have found no way to wash our dirty hands. We have hidden them behind our backs, we have shoved them into our pockets, but at last, when confronted with showing them, we have had to confess that they are unclean. Wash our hands, O Lord, but even more, wash us so we can become clean within. There is not one of us who can stand the torment and burden of our guilt, but you are eager to take our brokenness and miraculously make us whole. Therefore, we submit to you our lives — just as they are — to be made new by your love.

Hear the needs of every individual assembled in this hallowed place. Make sensitive our minds and hearts to the direction of your will, that our joy may be made complete and your name glorified and honored. Whatever its cost, O God, may we never fail to serve you.

In the name of our Christ, we pray. Amen.

73 O glorious God, how grateful we are, as Christian friends in _____ (*name of community*), that we can come together to worship you. How warm and satisfying are our greetings. How beautiful our mingled voices as we sing our favorite hymns. How moving that we who represent different traditions and creeds — rooted in the distant past — may in freedom discover a way to come together in this place today. We wonder how our love and appreciation for one another will grow as we faithfully remain open to your will for our common faith. Guide us, Holy Spirit.

We are grateful for those who shared their lives with our Savior and Lord in the first century. Often we see ourselves in their experiences. We are joyful when they succeed in living the faith, but sorrowful when they fail. We are angry when they behave selfishly or stupidly — only to discover that these same behaviors in us produce the same anger. Enable us in these coming weeks to grow in faith as we become reacquainted with our counterparts of the first century. May their faithfulness become our faithfulness. May their failures be our warnings. May their hopes become, in fact, our joy.

We are mindful of our friends and family members burdened with illness or sorrow. May they find in your presence every resource they need. We lift up to you our concerns for the hungry and poor of our community and world. Make effective our efforts in response to their needs. These words we offer in the name of our Lord and Savior, Jesus Christ. Amen.

74 We are grateful, God, for the opportunity of our community Lenten services. Sometimes when we are immersed in our individual ministries, we feel that we are your only witness in _____ (*name of community*). Then it's a source of relief and a surge of joy to rediscover that we are not alone. There are other steady witnesses at our side. We are appreciative of our various heritages. Each of our traditions was formed in a time when earnest souls looked at you in some unique way, then set out to tell others how you revealed yourself. As a consequence there are beliefs and practices that we hold and perform very differently. Yet, how marvelous it is that we can come together to worship you and experience a common bond in the name of your Son, Jesus Christ.

Help us in these days to keep our eyes upon the empty tomb. We serve a risen Savior. We are not a people of shame and sorrow. We are people of hope and gladness. We are not a people who stand at the side of our Lord's grave weeping for what might have been. We are a victorious people for we know that death is not our prison. Through the resurrection of your Son we have been set free. Our joy is boundless for it comes from you.

We thank you, God, for we and our world neighbors have been given one more chance at peace. Slowly, tentatively, the combatants in _____(*name of world location*) are beginning to put away their weapons, and the nations of our world are breathing a collective sigh of relief. We're not unmindful that violence, terrorist activities, and raw hatred still abound on our globe. But we hope to seize each opening for peace, and in faithfulness to your will reveal something of your kingdom more vividly than ever before.

Hear us as we confess our sin. Cleanse us of all our evil and keep us on the path that leads to you.

In the name of our Master, we pray. Amen.

75 We wonder, O God, our King, what you felt on the day of your Son's triumphal entry. As human beings we imagine that you might have been proud of him. Your Son was being cheered. In celebration his path was covered with clothes and branches. "Hosannas" filled the air. But then we speculate that as God, the omniscient one, you would see more in that event than we would. We would have settled for the surface jubilation. You wouldn't have stopped there. Your mind would have probed beneath the distracting sounds and activity.

Less than a week later, the crowds shouted to Pilate, "Crucify him!" Did you weep, O Lord? Or did your sorrow begin in the garden when you insisted he drink the "cup"? We like to think that if we had been there, we wouldn't have shouted for his death.

We imagine that with all our sophistication, our knowledge of mass communication, our cleverness with words, we would have kept Jesus, the Savior, from harm and ushered him into his kingdom.

But you know that it wouldn't have been our electronic gadgetry and communication techniques that would have failed; it would have been our hearts. Fear is fear. Self preservation is to be defended at any cost.

So in our saner moments we come to you in the posture of confession. We seek your pardon and take confidence that we will be heard.

We shall not weep, "If only, Father, if only it could have been different." For it can be different. The difference is what happens inside each one of us. For we can welcome Jesus Christ the ruler of rulers into our lives this very day. History can be rewritten within our hearts. Hosanna! To our Savior and King, Hosanna! Amen.

76 We still gather along the streets, our Creator, to cheer our heroes — be they military leaders, sports figures, or astronauts. In cheering them we keep alive our dreams that hard work, persistence, and excellence still yield success and victory. So we applaud the heroes and we applaud ourselves.

Was Palm Sunday enjoyable for Jesus? It seems it was a lark for the shouting crowds. It was something they could do in the hope they had found the military leader who would step forth and score a victory over the hated Romans. Perhaps this man, they speculated, was the man.

Or was Jesus sad — he had cried for Jerusalem a little earlier — for all its inhabitants kept looking for the triumphant life in all the wrong places.

We wonder what your Son thinks about us. Does he weep for us? Is he proud of what we achieve, or does he wonder why we don't turn to him for something more?

What love he offers, and forgiveness and hope and faith! However, we don't always receive his gifts, because of our reluctance to turn to him.

In the back of our minds, we know how much we need him. But our pride whispers to us, "Well, let's tough it out a little longer. You don't want someone else telling you what to do."

Our God, through the love of your Son we come to you, for our need is great, and unbridled pride is a treacherous enemy.

For those on our prayer list we seek comfort, wisdom, and strength. We seek for them an awareness of your presence and a reliance upon your faithfulness. In the name of Christ we pray. Amen.

Palm/Passion Sunday

77 Palm Sunday, heavenly Being, reminds us how quickly life can change. First the crowds of that ancient day shouted, "Hosanna!" in celebration of your Son entering Jerusalem. Then, within a week, the crowds shouted for him to be taken from Jerusalem and killed. We can easily imagine how his disciples and loved ones become confused and uncertain by these traumatic events. Who could — or can — make sense of them?

Abrupt switches and changes give shape to our lives as well. We go to work on Monday, on Tuesday we are unemployed. Today we feel robust, full of enthusiasm — tomorrow we may be taken to the emergency room fighting for our lives. Today we are well fed, tomorrow we may be hungry. Once we thought we were financially "set for life," but life took some unplanned turns and now we need to become pinch-penny frugal.

Spirit divine, enable us to expect the unexpected. Let us question any description of tomorrow that fails to include mention of the cruel and frightening sweep of change. Tomorrow — as close as it is — may be very different from what we anticipate today. Change remains the certainty of our days. Only in you, Lord, do we find the constancy for which we search. For you have been who you are even from the day of Moses, when you taught him to say of you, "I am that I am."

You are at the center of life's meaning. All else we have discovered is ephemeral. How grateful we are for your trustworthiness. Everything else may leave, but you remain.

We pray in the name of our Master. Amen.

78 Eternal Spirit, we express our gratitude for the service that Joseph of Arimathea and Nicodemus performed for Jesus on the day of his death. Nearly all of Jesus' disciples fled when Jesus was brought to trial, pronounced guilty of blasphemy, and nailed to Golgatha's tree. In the vacuum left by the disciples, came two men who were more closely identified with the staid religious community, than with this seemingly new, radical movement. Yet at the critical hour, they alone stepped forward so that the Master's body might be given a proper preparation and burial. Perhaps they were simply doing what the law required, but of all the people who witnessed and/or took part in Jesus' death, they were the ones who gained permission from Pilate to lower our Master's body from the cross that they might properly prepare it for burial.

Nicodemus and Joseph of Arimathea were less than brave in the earlier days of their relationship with Jesus. While they saw new possibilities for their faith in Jesus' teaching, they failed to commit themselves to this young, insightful teacher.

Who of us, O God, do not have regrets for failures in our earlier days? But who of us would now accept a task that would honor our Savior? It need not be a responsibility so important that it draws public acclaim. Let it be an undertaking that aids in a simple way the telling of the "good news." May the joy we feel from our labor, be its own witness to the faith.

We thank you for Joseph of Arimathea and Nicodemus who did the right thing at the right time. We don't know what price they may have paid for their caring act. But we do know how much we admire their devotion to duty.

May we do likewise in the name of Jesus Christ. Amen.

79 O Giver of Life, crucifixion in first century Israel was a grizzly business. At least that's what we think when we consider the centurions. Unhappily these particular soldiers had drawn the duty that stretches through the noonday heat. There was no relief from the sun, the shrieking crowd, and the agony of approaching death.

God, must we come to the cross?

However, for some, that day was immeasurable relief. The council, the high priest, Caiaphas, the Roman Ruler, Pilate, were glad to have Jesus off their hands. The sooner death came, the sooner he could be buried and the sooner they could return to life as usual.

God, is it required of us to watch until he draws his very last breath?

The cross, that day, was unrelieved pain. There was no solace for Jesus, his family, his remaining disciples, and the faithful attending women. How could he have been brought to this moment? What miscarriage of justice ordered him to this crude instrument of death? What hatred and fear shaped the minds of men who now took pleasure in witnessing Jesus take his last shuddering breath.

God, do we need to watch his nearly sightless eyes can scan over us for some measure of support and understanding, which we are either unable or unwilling to give? Can't we just go home?

Actually we can't go home that easily. Our leave taking is more complicated than that. For in our heart of hearts we want to tarry there. This broken Jesus is dying for us that we might escape the wretchedness of a sinful life and the finality of death. He has accepted this ghastly deed for us. This is his love for us. As those who were held by the final agony of his sputtering life, we cannot leave. We dare not leave, for it's not only his life that is at stake — it is ours as well. He is dying for us. We cannot simply choose to walk away. In his holy name we pray. Amen.

Easter Sunday

80 Some of us, dear God, have celebrated Easter twenty, forty, sixty times or more — and it has yet to lose its impact. We may remember some Easter celebrations more than others, but those memories don't dim our looking forward to the next one, which in some strange way seems to be our very first.

That we cannot fathom Easter's full meaning, doesn't put us off. It only adds to its extraordinary appeal. Easter remains at its essence a mystery. Yet it brings to us a simply told story of Jesus dying in our behalf and rising triumphant over death that we might have life eternal. We need dig no deeper to know of his glory.

Our hearts were touched the other day by the news of a fourteen year old boy who rushed out onto an expressway to rescue a stray dog. Unfortunately a car struck the boy and claimed his life. A father also lost his life in an attempt to save his family from a burning house.

If these incidents bring tears to our eyes, how much more we should be moved by what Jesus did on our behalf. He went to the cross, for it was his Father's will. This was the only way we could gain access to his Father. It staggers us when we consider someone's dying for us.

Heavenly Parent, we are grateful for your love. We bask in it. We claim the joy it brings. In turn we send our love to you. We pray in the name of our Lord Jesus Christ. Amen.

Easter Sunday

81 Our heavenly Creator, giver of our Master, Jesus Christ, we praise your name.

It was an Easter long ago when we children were in competition with each other, to see who had the prettiest dress or shiniest shoes. If we wore nothing new we tried to stand behind others acting as if we didn't care. The day of your Son's triumph became for us a day of pain and embarrassment.

Later on, Easter became a mystery. We discussed the possibilities of your Son's rising from the dead. Since we were a part of the church, we dutifully concluded that he had. But in secret we wondered. Then we tried to understand his ascension. We didn't want to be laughed at by the "learned" people outside the Christian community. How we wished to have the truth written out in large letters.

On an Easter closer to mid-life, we were surprised to discover that our earlier concerns about our appearance and the truth about the resurrection and the ascension no longer plagued us. They had become empty issues of a forgotten time. We were now concerned with who we were, what we had become — in brief, the meaning of our days. What had God expected of us? What had we expected of ourselves? Time was slipping by and if we were to make our mark, we had best move quickly. Eternal life was no longer a matter for debate, it was a matter of faith.

Here we are again, God. Our life's journey has been simplified. It's your love of us and our love of you that matters most. We simply want to be faithful. All else falls lower on our list of priorities. The resurrection now anchors our unquestioned hope. We are stunned to recognize the truth of it.

The headlines of our newspapers and the lead stories on the evening news shatter our thoughts and scuttle our emotions. But if we wait, if we wait, it is your love that rises into view and that's what lays claim to our hearts. What else is there?

Thank you for the Spirit's intercession. Amen.

Easter Sunday

82 Our God, if we had been at the empty grave with Peter and John on that Sunday of Sundays, how would we have reacted? Would we have believed immediately that Christ had risen from the dead? Or, like some of the persons of the first century, would we have waited until we had further evidence before speculating on his resurrection? If Jesus would come to us as he did to Mary Magdalene, would we be swept up by surprise — and then unbelievable joy?

Today we search for truth through scientific methodology. We don't take what we see as unquestioned truth. We want other corroboration than what our senses tell us. We nearly always want to conduct other tests and get the opinion of one more expert.

But certainty of our Master's rising isn't going to be proven or disproven by more tests or the testimony of additional experts. The decision we need must come from within us. It will be formed by the yearning of our hearts and the common sense of our minds and the daring of our spirits. Proof isn't possible, but belief is.

Therefore, we don't so much look for reasoned argument as we do for courage. We don't so much need interlocking paragraphs that lead us to some inevitable conclusion, as we do a leap of faith prompted by the yearning of our souls.

By taking a dare, what a morning this becomes! Death is no longer our tyrant, nor our end. It is a gate to a life — so testimony affirms — that is far greater than any we have ever known. And you, our Savior, bring us this life through your matchless love. May your name be praised forever. Amen.

Easter Sunday

83 Our Creator, we thank you for the gift of your creation. Soon we will stand on the threshold of spring, that time of miracles when new life bursts forth from tree and earth. Even now we see the swelling buds preparing for that day of light green leaves and delicate white blossoms. Already we find some eager plants pushing through the cover of winter, searching for warmth. How magnificent is your creation!

We remember the springs of other years; we recall how the plants and trees revealed themselves. We have not forgotten the musky odor of overturned soil. Nor do we take for granted the wonder of a tender shoot emerging from the hardened seed. Even so, each new spring fills us with an awe greater than we have ever experienced in springtime before.

Today we look upon an empty cross and an empty tomb. They are your symbols that point us toward new life. It was your Son who spoke the words we needed to hear. It was your Son who performed miracles that dazzled our eyes. It was your Son who died on the cross — but escaped the clutches of the tomb — to reveal that we are loved and worthy of life everlasting. Your Son is our eternal springtime.

It is through his name that we pray. Amen.

Sundays After Easter

84 Our Creator, how we enjoy the arrival of spring. Lush green grass rises in our lawns decorating our streets with home to home carpeting. Bird songs, silent in winter, now fill the air with enchanting melodies. The brown loam of our gardens and fields warms in preparation for the coming seeds and plants. The brilliant colors of jonquils, tulips, and hyacinths edge our flower beds and ring our trees. Who are we that you lavish upon us such splendor?

The air warms as the sun dispatches the winds of winter. The bursting buds and emerging shoots gather strength to thrust themselves into a new cycle of life. We rejoice in the plants that withstand the punishment of snow and freezing temperatures — already the delicate pansy blooms have appeared. We can almost hear the birthing sounds as all of nature welcomes the new growing season. We have been given front row seats to witness this breathtaking extravaganza. "O Lord, how manifold are thy works."*

Our hope rises with the advent of spring. We shuck off the debris of the past and begin our ascent toward the Son. We respond to your dictum of growth, God, and experience the joy of bringing forth the exquisite flower and nourishing fruit. Ours is the resurrection, not because we are beautiful or wise, but because it is your astounding gift to each of us. How manifold are your works.

In the name of our Lord and savior, we pray. Amen.

* Psalm 104

85 It is our intent, O Lord, to give you our undivided attention. As best we can we let the business of our lives slide off our shoulders. We coax our bodies to relax. We allow silence to have its healing way with our bruised and battered spirits. Deliberately we set aside all the explanations and defenses we use to put ourselves in a better light. Here we are, our King, humbled and penitent. We have eyes and ears only for you.

No doubt, God, you saw us this past week chastising the man at the parking lot for placing our car so far behind all the others. How indignant we were. In getting our car he wasted eight precious minutes of our time. And the lady in the doctor's office, did she really think we cared that her son visits her only once or twice a month? Let her go see other relatives if she is lonely. We could have defended a co-worker, the day before yesterday, but with work so scarce we didn't want to place our own job in jeopardy. We can't be too careful.

You know us, don't you, Lord? We wish we were more courageous and noble, less irritable and angry, but you see our record. So we come before you seeking your forgiveness. We have no other choice. Truly we are sorry.

Now, our Creator, guide us into better tomorrows. Enable us to see the possibilities of assisting and comforting those in need, regardless of their circumstances. May our ears hear their cries. May our eyes not turn away from their anguish. Most of all, help us to set our hands to tasks that will bring our sisters and brothers a full measure of dignity and respect.

We gather unto ourselves all that you choose to give us in this worship setting. Tomorrow we will be needed and we don't want to fail again the admonition to love those who share this earth with us.

Thank you for the skills and talents you have entrusted to our care. May we see joy on your face because we have been good stewards of your gifts.

These words we offer in the name of our Master. Amen.

86 Your creation, O Lord, is an awesome and astounding work. Sometimes it is so beautiful we stand stunned in silence. We don't move. With our entire being we want to take more of it into ourselves. Yet, at other times, your creation terrorizes us. Its sky darkens and becomes an eerie green. The rain pelts against our homes. Hail stones rata-tat-tat against our cars. And trees that we can't make quiver with our strongest effort, are tossed this way and that like a snapping whip.

Then in the aftermath of a storm, we wonder why it occurred at all. Is it creation's way of pruning out that which is weak and rotten? Is it nature's way of reducing the dominance of some species, while giving others a stronger foothold in the everlasting competition of the fittest? And what purpose is served when our homes are destroyed, and our possessions scattered over adjacent properties? What is the meaning of this crude, inescapable, and destructive event?

Is it endowed with some purpose that is beyond what we can know or imagine? While our knowledge of nature's growing seasons and its animals, birds, and fish increase, much still remains a mystery to us.

For certain we proclaim that you are God. We no longer hold onto an expanded idea of our own strength. We do not possess a power equal to yours. Rather we seek out the safest places to hide and hope that the storm's fickle route will not find us.

How great and wondrous is your creation, O God. You are omnipotent. Protect us in those moments of nature's wrath that intimidate us. Enable us to see beyond our present knowledge. Bring us to the truth that will open the prisons of our minds. Help us to realize more fully that whether we are strong or weak, alive or dead, we are yours. You alone are our God. We pray in the name of your Son. Amen.

87 Our Master, we tried going through life under our own rule. We said, "Yes," or "No," in regard to all matters. We determined how we should relate to the world around us. We alone fashioned the goals for our days. We believed our wisdom was all we needed to shape our lives and the lives of those dependent upon us. The only times we prayed were on those occasions when we were in grave trouble, but when the crisis passed we returned to our old ways.

Now we have come to the day when we have no remaining resource. All our ideas and plans are spent and in poverty of spirit we come to you. Our need is great and your love beckons. Even so, how can you love us when we have fallen out of favor with ourselves? How can our relationship exist simply on the basis of your grace and our promise of faithfulness? It's so staggering ... may we go over this again? ... because of your Son, our joy will reappear, our strength will return, and hope once more will accompany our plans for tomorrow. All we need do is confess our sin and believe.

Thank you, God, for your unending love. We are speechless with joy. We pray in the name of our Lord and Savior, Jesus Christ. Amen.

88 Our heavenly Creator, we deeply desire to live lives that will be in harmony with your plan for our world. Our best efforts do not always succeed. There are times when we fail miserably.

However, we choose not to give up the struggle to carry out your will. Nothing seems as remotely important. Your love, your justice, and your wisdom far outweigh all other social values we desire for our society.

In our country we struggle to find solutions for hunger, rampant disease, rebellion, flooding, prison uprisings, and suicidal cultists. And when solutions aren't quickly forthcoming we criticize those in charge. But in our quieter moments it comes to us that we are attempting to resolve situations that we don't understand and to a large degree can't control. We wonder what we will learn from these horrendous events. Will we turn to you for your wisdom? Or will we in anger, fear, and confusion decide to be stubborn, belligerent, or cowardly? Will we find some measure of understanding and resolution within the talents you've given us? Or will we turn away in helplessness? We are a needy people, easily given to frustration. This is a great testing moment. Enable us to learn from you the ways we need to follow, the confessions we need to make, and the commitments we need to keep.

These words we offer through the Holy Spirit. Amen.

89 O God, our Creator, we thank you for the warm love of friends, for books and videos that expand our minds, for musicians, actors, and actresses that stir our emotions, for public servants who struggle to be credible and effective, for parents who are devoted to their children, for young people who have set their vision toward a better tomorrow, for merchants who uphold high moral principles.

We are grateful, our Sustainer, that underneath the ugliness, bestiality, and furor that tops our news broadcasts and fills the front pages of our papers, there are millions of people pledged to the good life. Unknown and unheralded they submit themselves to the ways of love and wholeness as best they understand. We are beholden to them.

We thank you, Holy Spirit, for your presence in our lives. You are our great comforter. When our plans fall apart, our dreams disappear, and our beliefs become confused, it is so reassuring to know that you will provide us with what we need. We won't drift out of control toward some unknown port; relying on your wisdom, we will find ourselves and set out to reach the next destination in our life's journey.

These words we pray in the name of Jesus Christ. Amen.

90 A good portion of the time, our heavenly Spirit, we glide along on the surface of life. We get up, eat breakfast, enter our workday, eat lunch, finish our workday, eat dinner, go to an evening event or watch television and then back to bed. There may be a snag here or there, but nothing a little adjustment can't handle. And so we go through the week on automatic pilot. Weekends have their own routines, yet if all goes well — and it often does — we fly through Saturday and Sunday calm and cool. Life is "a piece of cake."

However, there are those times when we are pushed off our smooth track and minor adjustments won't get us back on. Troubled feelings erupt into our consciousness and we become irritable, angry, depressed, or sorrowful. We may try all the tricks we know to get back on automatic pilot, but none of them succeeds.

In mounting desperation we turn to family and friends trying to reach a calmer, deeper self. But we don't fully succeed. Then, at last, we come to you, God. Something has gone wrong and "business as usual" isn't going to put us back on our old familiar ways.

It is in these times that we discover how strong you are, how wise, how caring. What appears to be chaos to us becomes an opportunity for you to enrich our lives, heal our wounds, and deepen our understanding of life. How grateful we are that we can come into your presence.

It is our great joy that you are our God. And while our troubled times are never welcome, we have learned that they are the occasions that often bring us closer to you. Then our gratitude has no limits.

In the name of Jesus Christ, we pray. Amen.

91 O God, our Redeemer, we stand in awe of your grace. It is so immense we can not take it all in.

We should have known that your grace would be this way. Even a cursory acquaintance with nature overwhelms us. We look upon a rose and shake our heads in disbelief that such beauty adorns our simple garden. When we bring the rose inside our home we witness it transform a table in the corner of a room, into something elegant and regal.

We read a book and it take us to places in wisdom and knowledge that we didn't know existed. We listen to music and it lifts us above all that's tawdry to soar in some unknown heaven that we never visited before. We give our hearts and minds to our work, following the routines that are a part of nearly every job or position, to discover one day that we have erected something inside us that is enduring and strong. Behold, we — under your tutelage — have become a rock. We discover that our attempts to love have not been foolish. In some future day we will look into the eyes of a loved one and see there a magnificence, a caring, that we didn't dare hope would ever be shown us. Think of it, God! Looking into someone's love; and you, knowing it would happen all along. Dare we say the word ... grace!

Our words of thanksgiving come to you in the name of him who taught us how to love. Amen.

92 Sometimes, God, life seems so simple and orderly that we can't imagine why we were so troubled in the past. Then there are those days when everything and everyone seems so complicated that we wonder if we will ever cope with life.

We want life to be quick and easy. No heavy problems, just simple deeds, good health, unquestioned love, instant success, and unlimited money. But even as we say these things we begin to feel uneasy. A fourth grader could embrace this list without embarrassment, but we having lived longer know this wish list is not possible.

While we don't like to wrestle with hard problems, put up with physical suffering, or endure the pain of a broken relationship, we do admit that in going through such experiences, in company with your spirit, our lives recognize a wisdom, a love, and a truth that we would have never imagined otherwise.

To look into the eyes of someone we have hurt and see there a readiness to take us back; to look at someone who has hurt us deliberately and now behold him or her without bitterness; to look at someone with whom we have shared a great sorrow and now realize that the sun is about to burst over the horizon — what joy! What hope! What glory!

We pray in the name of the Holy Spirit. Amen.

93 When we are young, Our Creator, we simply don't think of death. It doesn't seem to apply to us. When we come to our middle years we become aware of death, but we do our best to ignore it. It's frightening. Slowly we realize that some day it will claim us. When we grow still older we make our peace with death. There are even times when we look forward to its happening. Not that we have given up on life, but it is the next great event of our lives, and on the other side awaits a life that we have been moving toward all the days of our existence.

Even with a growing acceptance of death across the decades, we are taken aback, stunned when it occurs among our family members and close friends. Our minds say they understand, but our hearts refuse to accept it and take us on a roller coaster ride of disbelief, sorrow, and loneliness. Our world changes dramatically and quickly, but we change more slowly. In between we shed countless tears and endure an inner pain that no palliative can reach.

Vulnerable and at the mercy of a destruction we cannot escape or defeat, we come to you. Steady and strengthen us through the weeks of our mourning and bring us once more into days of peace. Compelled by circumstances that cause us to reach out to you, may we gain a heart of wisdom and develop a compassion that we, in turn, may understand the broken hearts of others.

You, Savior, came to us anew through a death that was grossly unfair and cruel. One of the enduring promises of that death was a new life that will not end in death, but will transport us into a world we can only dream about. There we shall be with you, experiencing for the first time the fullness of joy.

We pray in the name of Jesus Christ. Amen.

94 Sometimes, O God our Lord, we are convinced that we see the truth of life. We are sure that we can walk a straight line to its door and we need make no reference to anyone else for we are confident that it is within our grasp. We thank you for those times.

But there are other times when we are not certain what the truth is. We struggle in our thoughts to reach a clear idea. Then having reached our desired goal, we find ourselves an hour later with muddled thoughts once again. Sometimes the definite, affirmative ideas of our friends make everything clear; then the clarity begins to disintegrate into a fog that clouds our vision.

Be patient with us in our confusion. Enable us to stay by our plan of reaching out to you — even when we are not certain of the direction. Remind us that you are forever, while our darkness and confusion are limited in time. Help us to see life open-mindedly, that we may be spared the imprisonment of habits that imprison us to one point of view.

As the sun breaks across the landscape at dawn, so does your spirit light up our minds to a new day in which we find truth once more. We pledge to be at your side in a hope — sure and certain — that you will faithfully open our eyes and minds to the endless truth you started giving us from the very first rustling of creation.

Gratefully, we pray in the name of our Lord and Savior. Amen.

Sundays After Easter

95 Sometimes words fail us, O Holy One. We want to speak from our hearts and minds, but what comes forth is drivel — tired old cliches — or worse yet, nothing at all.

We look at our son, our daughter, sitting across the room and we think how much we love them. But we back away from speaking our love for fear we'll embarrass them or ourselves. So we say something a lot safer, or say nothing at all and then feel bad about our cowardice.

We listen to persons criticize unfairly someone we know and admire, and anger rises within us, but we are reluctant to speak up in a social setting, where everyone is supposed to put on a happy face. So we swallow our anger and feel guilty that we failed a friend.

We want to make a point with someone who has authority over us, but we're fearful of jeopardizing our job, our community standing, our family love, so we tone down what we say because we choose to play it safe.

O God, how grateful we are that we can be who we are, say what we choose to say, without any reservations when we converse with you. We speak from our hearts, taking great joy that we can speak so plainly.

How rich and supportive are those times. Even when you confront us we are reassured, for underneath all the words is your unending love, your ready forgiveness, and your eternal strength. How great you are! You are our king, but when we enter your chambers you encourage us to be ourselves. Then we are supplied with courage so that on another day we may speak bravely to our friends and loved ones.

Hear this prayer, O God, our Sustainer. Amen.

96 Today, O God, our words are heavy for we are mindful of the pain that resides within our lives. While for each the pain is different, it is the same in that it steals our energy, undermines our confidence, and robs us of the certainty of our faith. Whether intermittent or chronic, physical or emotional, pain tempts us to believe that you don't care for us, and for whatever reason have chosen to punish us. Sometimes we think we are getting our just desserts; other times we are angry that we are being treated so unfairly. You know we rarely speak of these deep, deep hurts with anyone. Sometimes we even deny them to ourselves.

Grant us the courage to face our pain. Help us see that it is not only an interruption, or a distraction, but a guide, an arrow that points us toward growth, renewed life, and healing.

In guarded moments we speak of our anguish to others, and we listen to what they say. Other times we buy a book or a tape and apply the words to our lives, or we search the scriptures as best we can. But eventually all roads lead us back to you.

You are no stranger to brokenness. We have come to understand that you know pain in a different light. In some curious way it is your friend and, therefore, our friend. While other inner voices may tell us what we want to hear, Brother Pain doesn't lie to us.

We hold our pain up to you this morning. Enable us to understand what it wishes to convey. Transform us in its presence to live our lives fully, to know first hand that victory and joy can still be ours. Even in pain you are present, loving and caring for us through all the days of our lives.

Hear us in the faithfulness of the Holy Spirit. Amen.

97 It still disturbs us to recall those events, O heavenly Spirit. There, right in our homes, through the television's flickering images — who knows how many times — we've seen a man of one race beating/killing a man of another race.

Even though the criminality of what takes place seems to be so evident, still the justice system fails to see it. And the greater crime may be our timidity that permits and promotes such hatred and cruelty toward brothers and sisters of another color.

The only prejudice and hatred we can change directly is that which is lodged in our hearts. So we pray, first of all, for ourselves.

We confess we don't like thinking in these terms. Rather we like to think that there is no prejudice in us. For those of us who are free of such tyranny, we praise your name. But for many of us, when we are alone — with no one looking over our shoulder — and we begin examining our words, thoughts and feelings, we are embarrassed at what lurks just beneath the surface of our carefully managed behavior.

Forgive us, God. Help us drain this poison from our lives. If it isn't the Black, then it's the Asian. If it isn't the Arab, then it's the Hispanic. Someone, somewhere, feels our error-ridden, misspent wrath.

After our confession, help us discover how we can take that first step toward acceptance and understanding. Then may we continue with a second and a third.

Grant us the courage and strength to ward off the abuse of those who perceive that we've turned away from a prejudice that still owns their hearts.

Help us not to judge. God, we want to live and love. We want to enjoy life regardless who shares it with us. You are our Parent, and we are your children. What better goal can we aspire to, than reaching out to all the members of the family of man?

We pray these words in the name of Jesus Christ. Amen.

98 Sometimes, God our Sustainer, it is difficult to pray. Our thoughts are muddled and pestered by nagging little opinions that clamor for our attention. We start speaking to you in one sentence, only to find ourselves talking to you in another. These distractions keep stealing our concentration and before long we've forgotten what we were praying about.

How can we clear our minds? Should we simply pack it in for today and try praying tomorrow? Or should we keep on in our muddled way pushing through to the end of our prayer in spite of all the confusion?

We suspect that our dilemma isn't all that crucial to you. You've long since known that we confuse ourselves and this is just another instance of it. Perhaps we need to spend this time with you as best we can, not blaming ourselves, and go about the task of quieting our emotions.

It is so astounding to us that you are willing to abide our confusion, waiting until we can come to you in clarity. You are more caring of us than we are of ourselves. We judge ourselves so much more harshly than you judge us. Here we are chastising ourselves in your presence and your love is not altered one iota, though surely, we think, your patience must wear thin. O God, how we need you and cherish you. You are wisdom. You are love. Even in our confusion we can come to you.

Hear us as we pray for those on our prayer list. We can imagine you holding each one close to your breast so they will know how deeply you care for them.

These concerns we offer you in the name of our Lord Jesus Christ. Amen.

99 In the quietness of this place we hush the noisiness of our lives. We set aside the frenzy of our schedules to acknowledge that you are still our God, rather than the manufactured importance of our activities. Here, in this room, we reposition our priorities.

How good it is to be still. To let the music of the organ and the words of the hymns create peaceful places in our souls. How reassuring are the scriptures that reconnect us to a life that endures forever. How inspiring it is to worship with friends and family. On either side of us is a believer who, like ourselves, has decided to risk a faith-relationship with you, our Master. How that strengthens our commitment.

Something, or is it someone, stirs within us when we worship. We know there is a movement — imperceptible to the eye, soundless to the ear — that gathers up our talents and strengths to prepare us for the days ahead. How precious is this place. How priceless your children. How beautiful and supportive is the news of hope, the certainty of love, and the inspiration of faith.

We bring to you those on our prayer list. Though we are earnest in our prayers, that doesn't always mean we are wise. So we seek out not only your compassion, but your wisdom in behalf of our friends and family members. How you love them and us. Our confidence in your faithfulness is not shaken — you are our rock and our salvation.

We pray in the name of our Master. Amen.

100 O God, you have given us the hours of our days, the days of our weeks, and the weeks of our years. We thank you for these gifts of time. Enable us to use them wisely that we might glorify your name.

God, you have placed us over all your creation, the rolling fields, the high reaching mountains, the flowing rivers, and the sprawling lakes. For these gifts of place we give you thanks. Enable us to use your world so that your creation is protected and your children cared for.

Forgive us for misusing time and place. When we shorten our days by a wanton spending of health, when we use time for the advancement of our selfish goals, when we exhaust the harvest of the environment, when we disregard the gentle balance of nature, forgive us. We need to kneel before you with broken and contrite hearts.

Grant us a vision that will respect and care for the time and the place you have given us. When we look about the world we see how graciously you have provided for us. How rich is our environment and how plenteous is our time. Grant us wisdom to avoid pride and to seek how best we can serve you and your children about the globe. May we find our pleasure in serving you.

We pray in the name of your Son. Amen.

101 There are times, our Creator, when we wish we could be children again. Not that we want to live life over; rather we want to experience the simplicity of the love, the honesty, and the faithfulness we once knew. Things seemed clearer then.

We have grown up and become sophisticated and, unfortunately, wary. We say the right things, at least we think we do, but very carefully we're watching everyone. We don't want to blurt out something and be thought a fool. As a consequence, after we decide that the simple, straightforward response would be appropriate, the moment has passed us by. How we yearn to be spontaneous in certain crucial moments, but a lifetime of playing our cards close to the vest has taken its toll.

So we turn to your Son, choosing to model ourselves after him. In him we see the courage to meet our need or another's need in spite of the repercussions among family members and friends. We want to strive for a love that will show itself, just as it did in our Master.

And we want to show our love to you, dear God. We want a smile on our face and a liveliness in our voice when we come to you. We don't want to be hidden and cautious, but warm and open.

Enable us to speak honestly. It matters too much for us to come to you in some stuffy, outdated way. We want to be real in your presence. In this regard let us be your Son, in whose name we pray. Amen.

102 We are mindful today, our Healer, of our friends and family members on our prayer lists: ...

We pray for those who are confined to their beds, whose activities are limited to the basic acts of survival, and whose ability to recognize family members is uncertain at best. We pray that in their mysterious, fog-bound world that they will still cling to some awareness of your presence.

We pray for those who have been severely limited from the sudden onset of illness, the steady advance of a life-threatening disease, or the relentless pursuit of age. How frustrated they become, how frightened, how devalued, and how burdened. Even in these experiences may they know that they have high value in your eyes and that your love will never turn away from them.

We pray for those in the prime of life, who have been confronted by illness or accident, and now wonder if they will ever return to their work, or be able to contribute to their families. May they in these unsettling, threatening moments find that strength and wisdom that you have so generously placed within them. If they fail to return to life as usual, we pray they will yet succeed in adjusting themselves and their families to the world that is. Your Spirit is not limited to the boundaries of our thought.

We pray for those known to us within our friendships, families, and church, who, though able to enter into the daily routines of life, struggle in continuing battles with a brokenness of spirit. They are the walking wounded. We seek for them healing and comfort. May we remain sensitive to their quiet struggles.

How grateful we are that we can turn to you. You who enables us to rise from the most wretched of circumstances, to find the wholeness, joy, and hope you have buried in the very essence of our lives.

Hear our words of gratitude through the name of Jesus. Amen.

103   O God, our King, it is clear to us that our world, our nation, our neighborhoods are filled with people in great need. Some are ill and need medicine and a physician. Some are destitute and lack the most basic of all resources — food and shelter. Some are unemployed and don't have the job skills for even a simple task. Some are devastated by crime — having been beaten, raped, robbed, cheated, kidnapped — and they live their lives in fear and hopelessness. Some are caught in the tides of political change and haven't the knowledge or influence to bring about a difference in their lives. Hundreds and thousands in these straits have given up, resigning themselves to a painful way of life.

They need not be defeated. You are their God. Your kingdom is in force, your rule is compassion and justice. Your faith, hope, and love endure forever. The life you have given them is not limited. They can stand tall, for your truth is like a foundation stone that will support them all their days.

Today we consider how we can aid those who are in such great need. Sometimes we like to dream how we might become a part of some gigantic force for good that would sweep away all manner of evil and enable thousands of people to take up their lives filled with unlimited hope and success.

Please don't take from us the pursuit of our dreams, but enable us to see what we can do right here and now to meet the real needs of real people. We lift up to you who we are, what we have, and what we can do, to carry on a ministry to others in keeping with your will. Let us not despise the size and the scope of our gifts, but rather honor what we can do in your name. Enable us to be faithful to the tasks and opportunities that are set before us.

We pray through Jesus Christ, our Lord. Amen.

104 O Sustainer of Life, we turn to you in confidence that you will hear us. At those times when we have only muddled words, when we cannot express what is in our hearts, your spirit ably speaks our words for us.

So hear us today when our words are buried deep within us. We want to express our praise to you, but we think of saying sounds so banal, so empty, that we back off in embarrassment. Everything we start to express is inadequate; therefore, we end up saying nothing at all. Please listen to our hearts.

We need wisdom for the living of these days. Often when confronted with opportunities, we mistake them for burdens and respond by using tired old cliches. What might have been exciting quickly becomes old hat. We've only succeeded in transforming a dream into a yawn.

Help us to speak the truth when we pray. Don't let us get away with our badly worn excuses. Give us the words that will help us to be ourselves in your presence. Please listen to our hearts.

Enable us to pray appropriately for those in need. Sometimes we don't know what to pray for loved ones and friends, who are troubled and ill. As a consequence we pray for healing when being released from life would better serve the person. Or we pray for someone's peace, when waging a personal battle would bring them to yet a greater, fuller life. Always we will best serve others by placing their lives completely within your care.

Lift up our words for us. We give you our hearts. Amen.

105 It was a morning last week, our Creator, when the sun, preceded by a multi-colored sky, rose with such a purity of light that we stood transfixed. In those moments we were utterly convinced that your creation was beyond our grandest dream of beauty and power. That day we entered into our activities filled with awe and hope.

Nature has long been your faithful cheerleader. Countless are the times we have been gladdened simply because the sun came streaking through the clouds. We never weary of looking at the plants and flowers of our lawns and gardens. When the harvest season approaches and we hold in our hands the green pepper with its satiny finish, the ear of corn with its perfectly formed rows of kernels, the potato still smelling of the warm earth, and the pumpkin so bright in color, then we know happiness. We possess all the evidence we need to take joy in your world.

Then one day when the thunder reverberates across our fields, the snow piles high upon our streets, the tornado smashes our homes, schools, and churches, the flooding destroys all our possessions in one rise and fall of water — we are stripped of our hope for the future. This is when we need to dig deep into the nature of life to find there a wisdom and power that sustains even when the sun fails to shine, the beautiful flowers die on their stems, and our possessions are blown away. At last when we tally up all the experiences of our lives we become keenly aware of our dependence upon you — and you do not fail us.

It seems nearly impossible, but bright days and dark days are both occasions for the revealing of your love and truth. May your name be praised.

We come to you in the name of your Son. Amen.

Sundays After Easter

106 Gracious God, we search for new words to tell you how much we treasure worshiping you every Sunday morning. This is the hour — in company with family and friends — to recognize you as our creator and provider. Our need for you is unending.

The world whirls around us at a dizzying pace. All manner of things are happening today, and we haven't caught up with what happened yesterday. Often we have little or no way to influence these events — indeed, they influence us. As we listen to the news reports it seems that even powerful people are caught up in a web of defeat and destruction. It isn't difficult to feel hopeless and powerless. On the surface of things, we can easily conclude that there is no one in heaven and all things are wrong in the world.

That's why we anticipate coming here. Not as an escape from the world, but as a way to discover what is real and true for our world. Worshiping you puts things in their proper place. We are reminded of what is truly important. Here we become refreshed, renewed, and strengthened to move into the activities of our world for another week. Here we rediscover how much we love you, our families, and each other. Here we become clear about what we can do and what we can't do. Here we take the truth into our hearts. Thank you, God, for this meeting time and place.

We offer these words to you through the name of your Son, our Lord Jesus Christ. Amen.

107 Sometimes, Eternal God, we take our friends for granted. We see them often and they do and say the same things, they dress the same, they look the same — so we no longer give them our full attention. After a while they become a part of the background of our lives.

Then suddenly, or so it seems, something happens and we discover that a friend has changed considerably since we last saw her. "Whatever got into her?" we ask our neighbor.

We change as well. We're not the same person we were a year ago. We may look the same, we may even say the same things, but things are different inside us. When we reveal how we have changed our friends may be taken aback.

Help us, O God, to make peace with change — whether it's within ourselves or others. Life is movement and nothing remains as it is.

In some ways it would be easier if change were our enemy — the evil one. For then we could make an all-out effort to keep things as they are and hope to live happily ever after.

But life is dynamic. It is always in motion. The rose emerges as a bud, then opens to its fullness and splendor, then drops its petals and disappears. We can be sad about the rose, but we've learned that another bud will emerge, and then another and another.

Christ is life and light. The first century believers wept at his death until they learned that he had risen from death. Then he returned and returned again. Each time differently, but he returned. Once more they had life and light.

We like to talk about life as it once was. But we live by being attentive to what is happening in our lives today. Help us make peace with change. We pray in the name of Jesus. Amen.

108   There are times, O God, when we are convinced that we are doing the right thing and yet the result of what we do comes out the wrong way. At least, that's how it seems to us.

Perhaps we're impatient. Often we want results right now, when you are content to wait. Are we thinking in terms of days, when you are thinking in terms of months? Years? If this is true, grant us patience.

Perhaps we didn't do the right thing after all. We reviewed all the information at hand, we examined our motivations, and we talked the matter over with trusted friends — and with you! So how could we be wrong? Unless we did all the talking and failed to do our share of listening. We were so set on a certain outcome that we simply blocked out any other possibilities. If this is true, grant us an open mind, enable us to receive the truth however it comes.

Perhaps the results aren't coming out wrong after all. What seems like defeat or disaster now may be something wise and constructive in the future. Your Son's death on the cross must have seemed like the bitter end to his disciples. (Now we know he was revealing the true nature of your love.) Enable us to look again at what we believe to be all wrong — on the chance that it is something quite different.

It may also be that we have done the right thing and, even so, life is coming out all wrong. Perhaps there are no other alternatives. Has life played some cruel hoax on us? Watch over us, our Creator, that we don't turn to a bitterness and hopelessness that would compound our problems. As great women and men of the faith have revealed, we need to trust in you regardless what happens. You are our God, our Savior, within and beyond all that we experience. Grant us the strength that overcomes.

In the name of Christ we pray. Amen.

109 O God, our Creator, giver of our Lord and Savior Jesus Christ, have we told you lately how much we love you, for we certainly have been neglecting others. We awake in the morning to a dew-covered lawn, reflecting the sparkling, clean rays of the sun — like crystal dancing a thousand points of light upon our walls, and we say nothing. At best we offer a grudging "good morning" to our family. Shouldn't we begin to wonder why they have stayed with us across the years? We set our hands to our work, the duties that are ours, and below the grousing of "all we have to do" we are pleased that we are needed, but we keep it to ourselves. We show up at work, redecorate a room, write letters, drive a neighbor to a doctor's appointment or give a friend help with his garden. Then we feel good about ourselves, but we tell no one, not even ourselves.

Our Creator, what a glorious God you are. You have provided for our every need. You have given us a world filled with splendor and all we need do is live in keeping with its nature. You have bestowed love upon us, which we can take into our hearts without measure, if we but open ourselves to your will. Your love heals, inspires, energizes, and crowns us with a joy we can scarcely believe.

We love you, Lord, not only for what you give us, but for who you are. We love you not only in the good times, but in the bad times. We love you not only for who you are in days of celebration, but for who you are in days of sorrow and defeat. You are present in beauty; you are present when life turns ugly and grotesque. You are a God for all seasons.

We love you because you first loved us. Would we even know love apart from you? Because of who you are, we are rich people. All that we need to live the good life has been given us. Thank you, God, for the years of our lives. Now let us tell of your goodness.

We lift up to you the persons in our lives who are facing great need. Anoint them according to your will and compassion. Through the work of the Holy Spirit, we pray. Amen.

Gracious God we truly want to be "Christians in our hearts."

110 Gracious God we truly want to be "Christians in our hearts." If we are not Christians there, can we be Christians anywhere? Let the words of your scripture settle deep within us. Let the hymns of our faith stir our emotions. Let the devotion of our friends be a beacon light in our lives.

May our passions rise when we hear of our brothers and sisters around the world being starved and brutalized. May our tears flow upon hearing of innocent children being beaten and abandoned. May our love ascend unto you like the early morning sun moving ever higher into the sky. We want to be Christians in our hearts.

We pray, therefore, for wisdom. In a time when we are blessed with all manner of material goods, what is it we truly need? We live in a place that makes the insignificant become important, so how can we discover what is worthy of our attention? In a day when the word "love" is bantered about, how can we know what love truly means?

We want to be Christians in our hearts. We look forward, God of our faith, to the day when our thinking and caring is so in tune with yours that we automatically begin to assess each situation, each opportunity, in keeping with your will. What a day of glory that will be.

These thoughts we offer you through our Lord and Savior. Amen.

111   We turn to you, Almighty God, for your Son has brought you near. If once you were far away, you are no longer. Now we know that you are closer than the beating of our hearts. Your Son has provided this intimacy that even now — 2000 years later — we can scarcely believe.

All your children have great need of you, but many of us unthinkingly pursue ways that take us further away from you. In our fear of what is now known, we take foolish chances. Knowing so little about love and understanding, we strike out against what we perceive to be our enemy. And the more we strike out in opposition to our misshapened life, the more it strikes back confirming our mistaken view of your world.

We are afraid to walk alone at night. We do not feel safe even in our own beds. We wonder whom we can trust. So we sign papers before and after we have a car repaired, receive emergency health care, or purchase a home appliance. Children sue parents. People loot their neighborhood stores. Parents drown their children. Lovers shoot each other. Family members abandon their parents and grandparents.

Therefore, we turn to you, Sustainer of Life, for your behavior and affection are always the same. If we find no comfort in our society, let us find it in you. If our culture fails to make sense, are you not our wisdom? If the nations of our world fail to bring killing to an end, we trust you to be our source of peace. If we fail to protect the innocent, aren't you the one to swoop them up into your arms? We will not turn away from your creation, for you have intended it to be our source of life. How grateful we are that you are who you are. How good it is that we can place into your care all of who we are.

We pray, in gratitude, through the love of your Son. Amen.

112 This morning, O God our Savior, we thank you for friends. For the people that we see again and again at the bank, in the grocery store, at the prescription counter, whose smiles and service we often take for granted. We're grateful for the friends we've made at work, within our extended family, and at school.

Especially do we thank you for our friends in the church. They are the ones whose fate is joined with ours. And we care for each other very deeply. In all likelihood, apart from our meeting at church, we might never have chosen each other as friends.

We thank you for our abiding friends who have come closer to us than a brother or a sister, who steadfastly stand by us through all manner of sorrow and joy. They are the friends we've welcomed into the most intimate corners of our lives and they've not failed our trust. When our lives are deeply shaken by illness, rejection, or death — these are the people we want to have at our side. They have no way of profiting from our friendship and yet they come at the time of critical need. With them we can say whatever is in our hearts without fear of judgment; with them we can share our dreams for tomorrow without fear of ridicule.

One of our enduring joys is answering our telephone to find one of these friends, only wanting to say "hello." Such a simple act. Such an uplifting moment. Such a wondrous gift.

How deeply touched we are, when we consider that our Master wants us to call him "friend." What a honor it is to be given such an intimate place in his life. We will cherish this love all the days of our lives and in all the tomorrows of your heaven. To Christ be all honor and glory. Amen.

113   O God, our Creator, we thank you for life — the gift you have given each one of us. Help us to experience and give ourselves to those qualities of life that include love, mercy, and justice; and to resist the temptation of seeing life through our pain and sorrow, as deceitful and meaningless.

We confess that we often assume our interpretations of life are synonymous with truth. When someone has used us spitefully, we jump to the conclusion that all persons are self-centered and hateful. When someone deceives us, we are tempted to think that no one can be trusted. When goals we have set become as ashes under our feet, we assume that all of life is hollow, a chasing after the wind.

In our more reasonable moments, we admit that our viewpoints may be wrong. Then it is we see that some people live by trustworthy qualities, qualities that are positive, creative, and rock-like. A man contemplating suicide found in his daughter, reaching out to him, a significance that he couldn't ignore. That man grew in strength and wisdom. A lady despairing of her relationship with her husband, dared to believe in the love she first knew with him, and found it to be a key that opened the door to a renewed and uplifting relationship.

Grant, O God, that we will be able to endorse life in all its fullness. May we never — out of fear or anger — choose to hide behind negative responses to life that drive us away from ourselves, from each other, and from you. Undergird our faith that life is designed to bring its participants meaning and joy. Make us sensitive to your Son, who though he lost the life of his body, did not lose the life of his spirit. He received his strength from you and remained faithful to the end. So may we respond to you, this day and forever. Amen.

114   O God, our Creator, from your breath we were given life, from your soul we were given freedom, from your word we were given truth, and from your heart we were given love. Hear us as we come before your throne.

O Lord, help us overcome the barriers that separate us from one another and from you. Teach us how to forget past achievements, lest our boasting erect a wall that cannot be climbed. May we become able through your strength, to let past defeats and grievances remain in the past. Above all, help us to change that self-centered portion of ourselves so that it may be a channel to receive all people and not an excuse to reject them.

Words can never express, O God, what it means to us that you sent your Son into our lives. To know that he felt the ache of tiredness that comes with a hard day's labor; the temptations that lure and pull at selfish motives; the full, bitter sting of complete rejection that breaks the heart, and yet did not succumb to self-pity or hostility, is for us an open door to hope. Help us to receive him who alone gave us the victory to overcome the destruction of life.

We thank you for the members and friends of this congregation who give themselves that your good news might be proclaimed in this place, at this hour. May their lives be blessed in their labor, in their devotion, and in their faithfulness to you. May all our lives be bound together by your eternal love so that your will may be accomplished on earth.

Bless all who worship you this day. May their lives be made whole, we pray in the name of Jesus Christ. Amen.

115 O God of indescribable grandeur, to you we raise our words of praise and adoration. We marvel at finding you in the towering mountain at a distance and in the exquisite beauty of the flower at our feet, in the wisdom of ancient literature and in a child's innocent question. Regardless what avenue we pursue, you are there. You are implied in every challenge we face. You are the foundation of every answer we discover. Your greatness exceeds all descriptive words.

We gratefully speak your name, for you have shared your love with us. We come to you with cheeks stained with the tears of failure and despair and you carry us onto a safe place. You chide us about our pride until we confess the silliness of our behavior. You bestow honor upon us, never belittling us nor making fun of us. We are overcome by the magnitude of your love.

We gratefully speak your name, for you share your hope with us. In a time when the evil of our world seems to have gained control over the destinies of all people, your voice declares that you are ruler yet. Though the problems that confront us seem insurmountable, the resources your hand provides make us equal to the task. A light shines because you are interwoven into the history of the human race and this is your light. It is the symbol and promise of our hope.

Forgive us, gracious God, for thinking more of our own needs than of your ability to meet them. Restore to us a right vision of the life you have entrusted to our care.

This is our prayer offered in the name of our Master. Amen.

116 Eternal God, the hope of every soul, strengthen us in this hour of worship. Take us to that rock that is beyond the reach of our enemies. Be, O God, our high tower that we might be free from the sins that pursue us.

Sweep clean our vision, O heavenly Guide, that we might clearly distinguish the truth from the untruth, the high from the low, the clean from the unclean, and the enduring from the transient.

May we, through your guidance, be able to set aside our confusion and bewilderment and find the path where your word is a lamp to our feet.

O Lord, may our faith in you increase. Many times darkness creeps in because the events of our lives are so overpowering and imprisoning. The weight and burden of our existence becomes nearly too much to bear.

We cannot understand why death visits when it does, why hardship continually comes to the same life, why your children mock and destroy all that is good, why we are torn inwardly by hatreds, fears, and anxieties.

At last the question, "Why?" keeps ringing in our ears until we strike out at someone, run away, do something, anything in an effort to erase the shadow that darkens and claims us.

Therefore we fervently pray for eyes to see you in all your splendor; to see the world as the good place you have created it to be; to see others as beings of eternal worth; and to see ourselves as your beloved children.

Lead us to that higher place beyond our ability to reach, but within your love to give.

Teach us the beauty of surrendering, so that we can stop our petty feverish ways, our rebellion against you, and place ourselves within the power of your truth. This prayer we offer in the name of your Son. Amen.

Taken loosely from the Psalms

117 Our Creator, your word speaks plainly to us about the seduction of money. Money, or any other form of wealth, has been a ruler of humankind through all time. Emperors, military figures, industrialists, and religious leaders come and go, but money often remains the "king of the hill."

Money is a god. We bow down to it because it promises to provide all we want. Money doesn't care what we want, or what we'll do with it when we get it. Money doesn't care what words we use, or how we rhapsodize about other gods or values — as long as deep in our hearts it is money we worship. It doesn't even mind our railing about the evils and dangers of money as long as when "push comes to shove" it is our bank balance that we treasure most. Money doesn't even mind if we are consciously unaware of who our ruler is. Money is very flexible. It doesn't require us to swear allegiance, to memorize a creed, or genuflect to any symbol or place. As long as it has our hearts, it doesn't care what other loyalties we may have.

Lord, we are slowly learning how dominating money can be. It can enable us to accomplish all manner of philanthropic goals. It is also the means needed to meet all that is required for daily living. It fuels a church's ministry and a school's teaching. Money can hire a highly skilled specialist to save a life, to turn around a failing industry, or to bring together the members of a dysfunctional family.

O God, bring to us the sensitivity to recognize when we have turned away from you to make money the king of our hearts. Forgive us when we use it as a guide to determine our worth or another's worth. May we be wise in understanding money's power, without allowing it to determine our soul's journey. Money, indeed, can make possible the grand dreams of a believer's heart, as long as the believer's heart is guided by your will, dear Lord. It is your Son to whom every knee should bow. It is in his name we pray. Amen.

118 Now, dear Lord, that the leaves have fallen to the ground, we've started to grumble. We try to rake them when they are dry and they crumble into little pieces. If we rake them when they are wet they cling to the grass or to our rakes. We've forgotten the shade they provided when they were green, or the artist's palette they became when they were orange, yellow, and red. Now they cause us work so we grumble.

The truth is that this leaf dropping is a necessary part of the tree's life cycle that leads to the budding of its branches next spring. But the trees now are dark, black, and death-like. They look like a pen and ink drawing silhouetted against the sky.

Some of us, our Creator, are in the dark, black phase of our life and we wonder if we are dying. Sadness fills our hours. Pain washes over us. We keep losing a winning perspective on life. So you can see how interested we are in the trees of winter. Anxiously we pull back from memory how trees look in the warm days of spring. We recall seeing a light, misty green color, almost imperceptible, that delicately danced across the outer edges of the branches. We can barely wait until those first full green leaves appear.

We remember, O God; we do remember! We know that the darkness, the blackness, even the death of our spirits isn't the final word or deed. You have chosen to bring us a bright color out of the night and a new life from death. So we reach out to grasp the hope of springtime. It steadies our steps, it invigorates us, and it grants us hope. You are here and you are all we need. In the name of Christ. Amen.

119 We thank you, heavenly One, for your presence. Your chosen people centuries ago turned away from you. So have we. Yet you made provision for them to return to you. So you have done for us.

It's embarrassing to pray time after time for forgiveness when we keep stumbling over the same problem. How long does your patience last? Is there a time when you say, "No more"? Certainly it is true that our patience with ourselves runs out. We become so angry and frustrated with ourselves for saying the same destructive things, doing the same shameful acts, and thinking the same ruinous thoughts. So we lecture ourselves. Then we set out to pray more, read the scriptures more, and perform more good deeds. We say to ourselves, "Now God will be pleased, for we have turned the tide; we've set our ship to sail for home."

Then we discover you are unmoved. Not angry, but strangely unmoved. You are waiting for us to ask for forgiveness, to speak from a broken heart — yet one more time.

Savior, now we know of your unending patience. Seventy times seven we approach you in bitter need and each time you take us back. We fall one more time and you help us to our feet. We feel worthless and you make it clear that we are worth your unfailing attention. How marvelous are your ways. How unmatched. How enduring.

We bring before you the needs of our congregation and community. Help us to understand how we can be your hands and voice in the midst of need. Hear our words in the name of Jesus Christ. Amen.

120 The violence of nature, our Creator, mystifies and terrorizes us. We don't understand the reason for earthquakes, tornados, and floods, or why our world needs to be literally turned upside down by nature's fury. We see no good purpose in the destruction of our homes and villages. We only see death, injury, and millions and millions of dollars in damage.

We speculate among ourselves that perhaps you might be trying to "tell us something." Immediately we think we are being punished for something we did or didn't do. Have we consciously mistreated our brothers and sisters of this world? Or is it that we have chosen to care for ourselves, while ignoring the needs of others? Have we turned away from you?

We speculate that these horrendous natural disasters just may happen by chance — that there is no rhyme or reason for such calamities. A hurricane may appear this week, but a similar event may not occur in the same place for 25 to fifty years. Can it be that our planet is on some kind of time table that we know nothing about? That it moves this way and that way, and produces this and destroys that by some hidden master plan? On one hand there seems to be no plan; on the other there is a plan, but it is unknown.

Either way nature's course seems senseless and cruel. But then we often think that when things don't go our way.

If we look for a positive outcome to our musing, we are driven back to faith. This holocaust of nature isn't going to be made sensible by our thought or our logic. It's purpose, if there is one, eludes us. We simply know that you are God and that you are at the helm not only of our planet, but of our universe and all other universes. We trust you regardless what happens. We offer our confusion and fear to you lest they devastate us. We look to you and speak of our faith in who you are and in what you do. We stand in a long line of your children: Abraham, Job, the disciples, Martin Luther, the Wesleys, and Mother Teresa who faced the awfulness of the unexplained and yet persisted in keeping the faith. You are our God and we are your people — so you have declared and so we believe.

We pray for all people who have lost loved ones to nature's raging. We recall the young couple standing beside a pile of rubble that once was their home, lamenting the end of their dreams. Help us to pray with assurance that their dreams will be resurrected.

Thank you, God, for being with us — even in situations we little understand and greatly fear. In the name of our Lord Jesus Christ, we pray. Amen.

121 Lord, what was it that was so devastating yesterday, that brings us here today so depressed and troubled?

Oh yes, we remember.

It started when we stepped on the bathroom scales and got so angry because we had regained the weight we had lost in the last several weeks.

Then we snapped at a family member when we didn't even know what was being discussed.

Then we spent fifty dollars for a shower gift — to make a good impression on someone at work — at the same time bypassing an opportunity to give to the Salvation Army.

It was a string of little things that became monumental.

We try to change, Lord ... often. It's so discouraging that all our efforts at self-improvement have so little effect. Will we ever do anything right? Our friends lose weight, listen and say the right things, and stay by their priorities. Why are we such fumblers? All the little things join together to create an eddy, a whirlpool that drives us below the water's surface. All our struggling doesn't work. Rather, we continue to mess things up and privately confirm that we are failures.

We get angry at ourselves for our failures. We become silent and withdraw from others. Isn't that what failures are supposed to do? If we are not worth our own love, how can we expect the love of others?

We have turned on ourselves. But we don't talk about this rebellion. We've hidden this knowledge in a small secret place in our hearts. We don't even want you to know.

Then one Sunday we hear ourselves singing:

I was sinking deep in sin
Far from the peaceful shore
Very deeply stained within
Sinking to rise no more

But the Master of the sea
Heard my despairing cry
From the waters lifted me
Now safe am I.
Love lifted me.

Help us sing these words from our hearts. How they save us —
what hope they create.

What a wondrous God you are. You see us for what we are. We
fall on our faces for the hundredth time and yet you remain patient.
We have hurt ourselves and you are still willing to comfort and
heal us. How can we praise you enough?

It is your love that lifts us, that wipes clean the slate and writes
of hope that will bring us to a new day.

We bring before you our great need, in the name of our Lord
Jesus. Amen.

122 Now, dear God, we enter the fall of the year. It's the beginning of a new school term. It's the return of Congress to Washington. It's the time for cool brisk air, football, changing leaves, last minute cookouts, and harvesting.

It's also the time for the same old "stuff." Some things remain oblivious to the calendar. Drugs continue to be sold on our streets. Prejudice continues to dominate our emotions and our wills. We still use war to achieve peace. Many of our brothers and sisters still can't read, can't work, can't sleep inside, can't eat one warm meal a day.

We turn to you, not only to ask you to erase our problems but to assure us that our effort and dedication will make a difference, and that we will please you and bring dignity to ourselves and to others.

You are the one who has breathed life into us. You are the one who has given us love, joy, and peace. Because you are love, joy, and peace, you are our eternal hope.

We see you in our Bibles. We hear you in our hymns. We feel you in our heartbeats. We talk to you in our prayers. We listen to you in our silence.

How our spirits soar, for you are at our side. We need no skill or knowledge. We need only faith to know that at last you are the creator of our days.

Thank you, God, for choosing to love us. We are ecstatic, for you are a great God, a joyful God, a victorious God.

Enable us to be diligent in our effort to overcome those evils that beggar us every day of our lives. We are on the winning side, so we shall act like winners. Hear our requests and strengthen our efforts to serve those who sorrow, those who are lonely, those who are defeated, and those who suffer. We await your grace in the name of Jesus Christ. Amen.

123 Your love for us, our Redeemer, stretches our imagination to the limit. It wells up from within — where you lodge in each one of us — until we are filled to overflowing. Our joy is complete, for your love continues and continues. We are like a tea cup trying to contain a rushing mountain stream.

You must have been within the prophet Hosea when he went to the slave market to buy back his wife who had become a prostitute. She had lost her beauty and had been cast aside. She had become a slave. A nothing. But Hosea took her back, not as a nothing, but as his wife.

Just so the father took back his faithless son, not as a hired hand, as the son requested, but as his flesh and blood. Just so the shepherd went back into the wilderness to find the one lost sheep. Just so the woman swept her entire house until she found that one lost coin. We are that coin, that sheep, that prodigal child.

Through your Son you enable the blind to see, the lame to walk, the possessed to be free, the sinful to be pardoned, the hungry to be fed, the stranger to be taken in.

To make certain we would understand something of the nature of your love, you insisted that your Son, Jesus, die an ignominious death so our sin, our turning-away, our turning-against would be canceled, so that we could stand before you cleansed and healed — saved at last!

We don't know how to thank you, except to let our tears run down our cheeks, to shake our heads in disbelief, and to lift our arms in adoration. We love you, for you first loved us. We pray through the grace of our Lord and Master. Amen.

124 O God, in whom we place our trust, how good it is to come together to worship you. How often the emptiness of our lives has been filled with fresh meaning because we spent this hour in company with you and your children. At best our understanding of life is woefully inadequate; consequently we have a deep need to come into your presence.

We are a people who seek for security in the midst of a world that is unable to offer security. We become frightened and worried as we try to shape our daily life to meet our needs. How difficult it is to face the knowledge that we shall always live in the atmosphere of change. It will always be the nature of our living, and the security we need will not come from the work of our hands, but from you.

This puts us to the task of trusting. O God, how reluctant we are to place ourselves totally into your hands. We don't quite believe that you are able to care for us. So we hold on to some critical areas in our lives and take charge of them out of our own understanding, for we are not quite daring enough (or else we haven't suffered enough) to leave them in your hands. How mischievous is our pride, for sooner or later we discover that we have great need of you to minister to us. Help us, O Redeemer, to venture out in faith and offer ourselves to you. Grant that we don't hold on to our prideful selves so long that we are unable to let loose.

Refresh our famished spirits, bring peace to our troubled souls, accept the offering of our service to your kingdom we pray most earnestly in the name of our Lord Jesus Christ. Amen.

125 Eternal King, how great you are. You have formed the universe with its countless stars, its unending distances, its numberless mysteries. You have formed the earth and all it possesses. The rushing, tumbling rivers are yours. The monstrous oceans and rolling seas are yours. The small contented lakes are yours. You have formed the hurricane that shreds our shorelines. With your finger you have cut and gouged great valleys and canyons into the face of the earth. You have formed the giant redwood trees, yet you are still the God of the fragrant rose petal and the common blade of grass. How great you are.

Incline your ear, O God. Hear us who penitently speak your name. The path of our lives has taken us from the mountain top to the thicket. We pray as we unite our souls with yours this hour, that we will find the path which leads to a better tomorrow. May we sense, as we come to the mountain top, that your grace alone has brought us there. And as we approach the thicket, that your grace alone will sustain us there.

Forgive us, Lord. Help us not to suffer under the illusion that we can fend for ourselves in matters of eternity. Protect us from misusing our gifts solely for our own ends. Accept us as your unworthy servants, use our brokenness of spirit as an entering place into our souls. Take what you can find within us and remold it into a new person, transformed through the name of Christ.

Be our constant resource in everyday routines. Undergird us by your love and judge us from your sense of justice and, at last, bring us into eternal fellowship with you. This we pray in the name of your Son. Amen.

126 O God, our Listener, some of us have difficulty praying, while some of us come by it easily, regularly, and with considerable profit. Others of us have written it off — though we may still bow our heads, mouth words, and go through the motions.

Some of us learned to pray in a world that was predictable and understandable, or so it seemed. Right was right and wrong was wrong and while a few voices spoke in opposition, the general consensus so heavily supported these ideas that they became eternal truths, undergirding our way of life. Today we live in a world that is unpredictable, confused, and in agony. Many of our images and words seem hopelessly out of date and irrelevant. Some of us, therefore, have given up prayer as that exercise of our childhood (was it predicated upon superstition and magic?) which now needs to be dismantled and set aside.

Yet a few — certainly there are more — cannot leave prayer alone. Some have continued to pray through victory and defeat, order and chaos, providing an anchor and a hope for the rest of us who muddle after our broken dreams in an uncertain world. Something (a spirit within us?) is restless to be in communion with you. It isn't enough that we are here alone, in this moment of time, it is essential we are here with you and each other.

We may need to learn to pray all over again. We cannot start from innocence, for we are no longer children. Our faces are creased with worry, our manner of living is anxious and fearful, yet our need to reach out in trust to you is no different than in the days of our youth. Grant us mounting courage to seek after you in faith. Such is our hope that we will not give up the quest.

Hear this prayer through the activity of the Holy Spirit. Amen.

127 Our Creator and Savior, we witness that your hand is un-
wavering as you guide the destiny of all people. In our triumphs
your power and wisdom can be seen. Even in the midst of all our
tragic defeats and sinfulness your purposes go forward unmarred
and unchanged. You accomplish your will through our love and in
spite of our fear. You are ever the same.

Our prayer today is for constancy. Without our understanding
why, some of our days are cheerful, smiling, and kind. Other days
are surly and mean. First we walk along a mountain pathway ex-
hilarated and joyful; then we are in a valley devoid of hope and
meaning. We don't set out to be so changeable and unpredictable,
Lord.

You know we have tried to set our lives on a steady, even keel.
We have vowed to remember the mountain top when we are depressed, and to temper our days of enthusiasm with the memories
of our defeats. Yet our ascents and descents rise and fall sharply
despite our best conscious efforts.

Therefore, today we offer up to you our fickleness and seek
out your Spirit, which is reliable every day, to enter our lives. Have
your way with us that we might be the useful and productive persons we were created to be. Let us find our steadiness in you.

We thank you that whether we are on the mountain top or in
the valley, you are with us. No mood of ours excludes you. No
quick change of our emotions drives you away.

Hear, dear God, the needs of your children as we lift up our
confessions to you. Bind our wounds, comfort our grief, strengthen
our resolve, and guide our footsteps. In the name of Christ we pray.
Amen.

128 Thank you, God, for the month of May. Silently green leaves waken and stretch to their fullness. The dogwood dons its garland of delicate blossoms and the lowly dandelion, unmoved by our rejection, throws its yellow-gold across our lawns and meadows.

The earth smells musky. It crumbles in our hands, feels warm under the sun, and welcomes the seeds to its bed. The drama of the seed — young plant, mature plant, harvest — is as ancient as time and yet we can scarcely wait to see it enacted once again. Each day we look for growth. It's a momentous occasion when one step leads to another.

The bush beans aren't just bush beans, the tomato plants aren't just tomato plants. They are enacting the story of a faithful life. They are portraying the gospel right in our backyards. There is death, birth, growth, and harvest. Our plants perform exactly as our Lord prescribes.

As we watch for growth in our garden plants, so we pray for growth in our lives. Teach us how to give up our present standing that we might become new. Enable us to have faith in our growth, lest we snuff it out to return to our old familiar ways. Aid us in developing a confidence in a good harvest — even as we admit that such a guaranteed result seems risky. Let our faith be in you. Thank you for showing us what is real in the living of our days.

We offer to you these words through the Lord Jesus Christ. Amen.

129 Today, our Savior, we are remembering the thousands of people who have been injured or killed from violent acts of nature, in our country and our world. Though we don't know them personally, we now choose to take them to our hearts as a part of our church family.

We confess we don't understand, O God, the necessity of tornados, hurricanes, earthquakes, and floods. We don't see how they are of any benefit. To us they bring senseless destruction and death. Our real question, beneath all the other questions we ask, is "Why do you permit such events to take place in your world?" If there are reasons for these calamities, or purposes served by their activity, we fail to see them. Whatever benefits there are, we speculate that they are far outweighed by their savage cruelty to your world and your people.

We don't fully understand your ways. You remain, in part, a mystery to us. We imagine that you don't see these events as we do. In your Word you reveal that whether we are dead or alive, we still belong to you. Also in your Word you teach that money, property, and "things" are not substitutes for placing our trust in you. We know that you attach greater importance to our loyalty to you, than to the amassing of power and wealth.

Perhaps you want us to know the full measure of our helplessness so that we will turn to you in unrestricted faith. Is it that you want us to know — once and for all — that belonging to you is far more important than anything, or anyone else, including ourselves? So it comes to us that you will go to any length to reveal the truth of life to us.

When our understanding and reason run out, we will hold fast to our trust in you. Though your world causes disasters we greatly fear, still we are yours. No violent tumult will wrench us from you.

Grant us courage, grant us wisdom for the living of these days. In the name of Jesus Christ we pray. Amen.

130 How grateful we are, gracious God, that you are with us in times of great difficulty. When our strength begins to wane, you are at our side to replenish us. When our nerve fails us, you are present to strengthen our will. When we cannot muster the wisdom needed to meet the demands of the moment, you generously supply us with your wisdom. Relying solely upon ourselves, we fail. Relying upon you enables us to complete our tasks and experience joy in what is accomplished. For your presence, we offer our greatest thanksgiving.

How grateful we are, God, that we can meet with your children in experiences of worship and instruction. When the tasks of our week pull us more and more into darkness, how good it is to come to your house and bask in your light through the faith of our fellow believers and through the presence of the Holy Spirit.

When frustrations mount because we can't make life conform to our will, how steadying and nourishing are the calm, wise words of your Word and the testimony of your children. When our spirits give way to anger and hostility, how eagerly we welcome the peace of your Spirit. The advice of your people enables us to proceed with a patience that leads us to healing.

How grateful we are that you are our God and that we are your people. Hear us as we lift up our prayer in the name of our Master. Amen.

131 Dear Lord, as you know, we respond in very different ways to rain. When it fails to appear over a long period of time, we watch in frustration as our lawns turn brown, our gardens stop growing, and our exposed soil rises in clouds of dust.

Then when the rains come we are so grateful. After a long cool drink, we can scarcely wait for the sun and the heat to return that we might see greener lawns and more productive gardens.

But when the rains stay too long, when the temperature drops, when the air is muggy, when stored items begin to show mildew and the earth squishes beneath our feet — then we become frustrated again. We lament postponed picnics, concerts, sports activities, and we fret because we can't mow our lawns.

God, Father of our Savior, you also know that we respond to you in very different ways. When your love comes knocking at our door, how delighted we are to let you in. You restore us to joy, place our feet on solid ground, and cancel out the guilt of sin that looms above our heads.

Sometimes we try to hide from your presence. We grouse because you ask for excellence when we would just as soon muddle along. We're fearful that you will punish us for our sin, cause us to follow a narrow path, and set us to tasks that we don't want to undertake.

This brings us to the moment of saying no to ourselves and yes to you. This is a very difficult choice. Our future will be imprisoned or set free by the decision we make. The quality of our lives is challenged. The words "yes" or "no" come with agony to our lips. O Lord, grant us the courage to clasp you to our hearts. Help us to move past the temptation of living only for ourselves. May the bravery of saying "yes" to you, bring us to a certain triumph and a redemptive joy in our tomorrows.

In the name of the Lord Jesus Christ we pray. Amen.

132 Summer is more than half spent, O God, and we continue to rejoice in growing things. Our vegetable and flower gardens are giving us nourishing food and glorious color.

Often, dear Creator, we don't think of you in the midst of our activities. But when we stop — even for a few seconds — to study the vegetable, the flower that has emerged from the soil, that only a few weeks ago was a seed, it is a quick revelation of joy and hope.

How orderly your world is. The seasons come and go in the same pattern. The earth, planets, and stars follow a very precise travel log around and in between each other. The animals and birds follow an inner clock that tells them when to leave one point to go to another — at just the right time!

Our Creator, just when we think we understand the orderliness of your world, you stun us with a tornado or a flood. You bring us a new insight into the make-up of your world, a new learning that scuttles our thinking of the past. Then we come to realize that we don't know all your ways. You live in a way that is different from ours. Your life is bigger than ours; your purposes include us but they also reach far beyond. Your power is awesome. Your ability to nurture and care bring us into experiences of joy and love we can scarcely imagine.

We become humble in your presence. We become quiet and in the silence we begin to learn who you are all over again.

In the name of Jesus Christ we pray. Amen.

133 O God, why can't we always be on vacation? Resting when we wish, swimming when we wish. Why can't we go on long walks every day just for the sheer pleasure of being immersed in the wonder of nature? Why can't we all be endowed every day with good health and a spirit of peace? Why can't work always be upbeat and successful? What's so wrong with a continuous diet of beauty, victory, and laughter?

Whatever our wishes for life may be, Lord, our experience reveals that there is also fear, struggle, pain, hard work, and defeat. Strange as it seems, when we look back across our lives, the times when we met adversity head-on provide us with the greater satisfaction, while the times of fun and laughter are harder to recall. Something about victory hard won endures.

In the scriptures we read of the conflicts, the jealousies, the hostilities, the long desert treks, the times of hunger and thirst of your ancient people Israel. We have also read of the torment and death of your Son. We know of the faithfulness of countless Christians who refused to walk away from their sacrifices. Our interest to know who they were and what they did never has been erased.

Where would we be today if the people before us had always been on vacation? If life had always been a lark, to whom could we turn in times of darkness? Party people don't have much to offer when life grinds us down in pain.

We resist saying, "Thank you, God, our Creator" for our suffering, but we can say, "Thank You," for being healed. It is most difficult to say, "Thank You," for those times when life falls apart, but we can say, "Thank You," for a hope that rises above disaster. We fight against saying, "Thank You," when we have been discarded, but we say, "Thank You," for your love that always includes us.

At last we may not wish to be remembered as "a good-time Charlie." Rather we wish to be remembered as a person who turned adversities and challenges into experiences of beauty and accomplishment. Thank you, God, for being with us in the "real" world.

These words we bring to you through the Holy Spirit. Amen.

134 We come before you, our Savior, just as we are. You, and perhaps only you, know what is happening inside us. You see our fear. You know what courage we need just to meet the challenges of everyday life. Our faces smile and our words are the same ones we've always used, but inside behind the bravado, we are hoping no one will see the uncertainty of our smile or hear the tremor underneath our words.

You see our worry. You know the true nature of our burdens. Sometimes, just by the way life unravels, we must adjust to a heavier load. But other times we take onto ourselves schedules that overload us, problems that can't be solved, and cares that rightfully belong to others. We confess that we cannot always tell which is ours and which belong to someone else.

You see our lack of self-forgiveness. You know how hard we are on ourselves. The patience we offer others, we deny ourselves. Life has become bleak, gray, unfocused because we have decided — day in and day out — to punish ourselves.

So we come to you, not from rational thought, but from overwhelming need. We are incomplete, but you can make us whole. We are weary, but you can bring us rest. We are wounded, but you can heal us. We are in darkness, but you can supply us light. What a transformation we can experience in your presence. How unbelievable is your grace. How glorious is your victory that overcomes our defeated ways. Now we stand taller. Now we step into tomorrow with confidence,

In Christ's name we pray. Amen.

135 Sometimes, dear Lord, we clearly see you in the behavior of others. We see you in the parent who sleeps on the floor by a child's sick bed, on the chance the child may need something during the night. We see you in a friend, who rescued us when we were being hit and kicked by hoodlums, and weren't you the one who gave a kidney, that life may be extended to another? Further, you were the parent who, in court, stepped in front of his son, to request that the sentence be placed on his head.

You were the one whose fingers played the "Moonlight Sonata" that stirred our souls. When fear gripped our spirit you appeared at our bedside to sing a simple hymn that quickened our faith. Certainly you live in the experiences of countless people recorded in the scripture, guiding us through the valleys of defeat and death.

In all these encounters we reach for words and meanings that we don't possess to describe how wondrous is your appearance in others. Hear us in our need. Receive our flagging words in the name of our Lord and Savior. Amen.

136 This past week, Creator God, when storms and tornados swept through our community four consecutive nights, we were once again reminded of our frailty. Homes, trees, churches, store fronts, and cars were bounced, broken, and blown away in a matter of seconds. Places and things we think of as unassailable were destroyed by the spiraling twister that dropped from the sky.

We pray for the members of a community church. How can we relate to the pain and sorrow they feel? Can we even imagine the destruction that now disrupts their every program and ministry?

Yet we know that you are still with them. Many of the signs and symbols of your presence in that church have been destroyed, but you are still there. In fact, you may be sought more often now than before and we pray that this will result in an even more effective ministry.

We are pleased to hear that members and friends of this church are uniting — closing ranks — as they set themselves to overcome this disaster, under the direction of your Spirit.

We pray for this congregation:

When sorrow weighs heavily, may there be a lighter burden.

Where hope seems faint, may there be a renewal of strength.

Where destruction has shattered dreams and plans, may there rise new dreams and plans.

Where suffering rules the day, may there be healing and joy.

Where defeat seems overpowering, may there be victory.

Hear our prayer, O Lord. Amen.

137 We come before you this morning, O God, out of deep concern for our world. Hostility, hatred, and fear have long been with us. They are wretchedly displayed in verbal attacks, physical abuse, murder, starvation, rape, prejudice, war ... there seems to be no end.

We vent our uncontrolled anger on women and men, wives, and husbands, mothers and fathers and defenseless children. Unable to cope with our own problems, we brutally attack family members, friends, and neighbors.

As nations we appear unable to roll back the prejudice and hatred that separate us. So we turn to threats of war, or war itself, claiming it to be the legitimate peacemaker. When we behave destructively, we offer what we believe are noble justifications, which convince no one, not even ourselves.

We desire peace, but bullied by fear, we turn to violence. We want friendship, but conditioned by half-truths and biases, we choose to live a lie rather than face the frightening task of trusting an enemy.

But not all is lost, dear Lord. You are still our God and we are still — regardless how tenuously we cling to your fatherhood — your children. Your truth guides us. Your love chastens us. Your strength supports us. Your wisdom corrects us. We face a grave danger, but we are not bereft. We do not stand alone; even death is not the end, but the beginning of new life. Lord, increase our faith.

In the name of our Master we pray. Amen.

138 Our heavenly God, you love us when we fail to love ourselves. You love us when we fail to love others. You love us when we fail to love you. We confess we are not always aware of the faithfulness of your love.

We behave hatefully and are unaware that your heart is filled with pain and sorrow. We fail to call upon your compassion; rather we choose to attack or run away. As a consequence we make ourselves prisoners of fear and hostility and yet you choose to wait patiently for us to return. Forgive us when we believe that we stand alone against the world, for, in truth, you are standing at our side all the while wanting to share your life with us.

Open our eyes that we might see you. Open our minds that we may understand how to learn from you. Open our hearts that we might receive your love and give our love in return.

We thank you for the children worshiping with us this morning. They bring us great joy and hope. We wish for them fun and happiness. Soon enough life grows somber and if we don't find joy when we are young, how will we recognize it when we grow old?

Accept the words of our prayer, Almighty God. Amen.

139 There are times, dear Creator, when we are sure we know what is right and what is wrong. We are so certain that we don't even consider any other information or opinion. We go our own way feeling that we have life within our grasp and even make fun of those who see things differently.

We come before you today not in arrogance, but ready to hear what you would teach us. We are thoughtful and reflective. We know that our strength, our skills, our money, our achievements ultimately will not win the day. We are vulnerable for something at the center of us is flawed. We have made harmful decisions. We have confused our wants as your will. We have ignored your wisdom in favor of our own.

We confess our wrongdoing. We regret our pride and seek your forgiveness. Somewhere within the sheltered valleys of our lives, sprouts of hope and trust are forming, reminding us that you are still in our world. You haven't turned away, your ways still prevail, your wisdom and truth continue. You wish for us freedom from sin and desire for us wholeness of body and mind.

We kneel before you knowing we cannot be compared to you. Our appropriate response is awe. We accept the gift of your love, little understanding why you so keenly desire to give it, but eternally grateful that you do. Thank you, God. Please accept our prayer in the name of Jesus Christ. Amen.

140 One of the limitations your creation places upon us, O God, is time. We cannot make it slow down or speed up; it moves inexorably at its own pace. We enter it at one point and we shall leave it at another. We have no ability to alter or change its character.

The only segment of time we know is the past, which we'll never experience again. We are always looking toward tomorrow, and yet we shall never enter it. The one segment of time that we consciously experience is the present moment — now. It is the only section of time upon which we can bring our influence to bear. All other time is beyond our grasp.

Help us to use our past as a teacher. May our reflection upon it grant us wisdom for the present moment. Help us to set aside the temptation to immerse ourselves in what might have been — or to plunge into the morbid game of "if only."

Grant us the spirit of faith and hope in anticipating tomorrow. Remind us that there is much more to life than waiting for the next event. Sometimes we think, "As soon as I see the doctor," "As soon as Labor Day weekend is past," "As soon as we get a new car," "As soon as my spouse apologizes to me," then — and only then — will life begin again. However, we cannot wait to live until then.

Therefore, grant us the courage to live now — today. Help us to grasp this moment — the only segment of time available to us — and use it for the eternal values of faith, hope, and love. Today we speak. Today we listen. Today we act. Today we live.

In the name of the Lord Jesus Christ we pray. Amen.

141 O God, our Creator, it must have been a grand and over-whelming moment when Moses brought the children of Israel the great stone tablets bearing the words of the Ten Commandments. It must have been a high moment of reverence when the priest read from the Torah that was so carefully written on a scroll. It must have been an eagerly awaited moment when the first century churches assembled to hear Paul's latest letter. It must have been a holy moment when the common man held in his hand, for the very first time, a copy of the scriptures in his own language.

Today no one needs to be without a Bible. No one. There are so many versions and translations that we can scarcely keep record. The number of publications confuses our minds. Even so, there are many who are without the scriptures. Some simply don't have the money needed to purchase one. Others may not be able to read. Still others have been denied any access to the printed word. Of course there are those who choose not to read it. Our ministry is cut out for us.

So we set ourselves to the task of proclaiming that the Bible sets forth the good news and offers a way of living that brings victory and joy. Especially it is good news for the person contending with a critical personal problem.

We thank you, God, for the Bible. For the place it holds in our lives. We thank you for those organizations who have undertaken the ministry of supplying scriptures to people around the globe. May we not rest until all people have the scriptures in their hands.

We pray in the name of Jesus Christ. Amen.

Pentecost/Church

142   Eternal God, as accustomed as we are to all kinds of people demonstrating on our streets, we find ourselves taking a second look at the people who gathered on the occasion of Pentecost.

First, they were on the street at 9 a.m. — that seems a little early to us. Second, though they were all supposed to be from Galilee, when they spoke it was in the languages of all the foreigners who were in Jerusalem on that day. Third, their unusual behavior was attributed to the Holy Spirit.

Lord, we know that some of us in the church are ecstatic about the behavior of the Holy Spirit. More of us are a little wary of what we hear and see. Who is the Holy Spirit? Will he ever require us to pray aloud on the street corner in a foreign language? If we, who are rather up-tight about all manner of public behavior, are taken aback by the event of Pentecost, what of the people who actually witnessed it? It is not a wonder they thought the demonstrators were drunk.

At least we have learned that the Holy Spirit is not defined or controlled by tradition. He moves in concert with truth, even if he appears to be odd or silly. He promotes reconciliation and joy, and he doesn't concern himself if we are embarrassed. All that he does leads to wholeness and health, even if the routes he provides take us away from the more popular highways. Once we become accustomed to his surprises, our confidence in his passion for love grows stronger day by day.

We offer these thoughts in the name of our Master. Amen.

143 God, our Redeemer, how refreshing it is to come again to this place of worship. This building was constructed and cared for by the generations that preceded us, that they and we might have a beautiful and safe haven in which to invoke your presence.

This room is unlike any other place we enter. Here we sing gospel songs and hymns that we rarely sing any other place. Here we pray together, which we seldom do elsewhere. Here we reflect upon the meaning of the scriptures and are given opportunities for spiritual growth not offered at any other public gathering.

In this room we let down our guard. We leave the strain of the past week ease from our bodies. Here we don't sit rigidly ever ready to defend ourselves, explain our behavior, or promote our accomplishments.

In this hallowed hall we unite not only with each other, but with all those who have gone to eternity, and who now form around us so great a cloud of witnesses. Further, while we gather here, other believers are coming together on the next street and down the road. We take strength from the church gathered and the church scattered.

This is also a powerful and purposeful hour. We come depleted and leave refreshed. We come confused and return clear-minded. We come feeling estranged, but go back to our duties cared for and loved.

May we receive our inheritance of joy and hope. May we pass them on strengthened and enhanced. We thank you, Lord, for our church. In the name of Jesus Christ we pray. Amen.

144   How good it is, our Savior and Creator, to assemble here this morning. Our presence here is our common witness to a faith that forever nourishes and sustains us. Whatever took place in our lives this past week, be it sorrow or triumph, we present these events to you for you can fashion meaning from them. You take our experience into your hands, as a potter takes clay and gives it symmetry, shape, and design. Otherwise these experiences may become meaningless or destructive.

It is our delight to sing together. Our voices mingled with those of family and friends give witness to our faith. The words describe the purpose of our existence in ways that are forever fresh and new. The music sinks deeply into our memories until one day we hear ourselves humming a hymn that warms our hearts, grants us courage, and inspires us with hope. Then we are unspeakably thankful.

What a joy, what a challenge it is to give attention to your word from the scriptures. At times your word is so plain that we cannot but understand. At other times we labor to understand your teaching. Often the scriptures, that we struggle to grasp, are the ones that have the greatest impact on our souls. Studying the Bible's timeless words is a certain way to salvation and wisdom.

We thank you, God, for this hour of worship. In the name of Jesus Christ we pray. Amen.

145 When, O Lord, did we first realize how much we love our church building? How beautifully it stands, ringed by trees that have been reaching up to you for decades. So pristine in its whiteness, yet containing all the warmth of home.

When, O God, did we come to know how important weekly worship is? We've come here when discouraged, doubting, guilty, and defeated. We've come here when happy, expectant, assured, forgiven, and victorious. Either way worshiping you enables us to place the elements of our lives in their proper order.

When, O heavenly Spirit, did we first become aware of how much we love all the people who come here to worship? If our friends are in their usual pew we feel assured. If they are absent we feel uneasy and incomplete and inquire of others where they may be. Failing to get any information, we call them as soon as we get home. How we need each other for the strengthening and understanding of our faith.

When was it, Lord, that we discovered that this place makes us aware of your presence more than any other? Most certainly you are with us all week — but here you come into sharper focus. Here we listen more attentively to your voice. Here we fall into deeper thought concerning your Son and his teachings. Here tears come into our eyes as we are reminded how central you are to all that we do and to all that we are.

Thank you, God, for our church.

We are especially concerned for the members of our church family who have unique needs this day. We pray knowing that your care will surround them. And that we, as your instruments, may also be called upon to encircle them as a witness to your love.

Hear our prayer through Jesus Christ. Amen.

146   Eternal Spirit, some New Testament teachings are difficult to understand. For example, today we are wrestling with the idea of being a holy people, a people set apart. We resist the idea of being holy, for we have great difficulty thinking of ourselves as virtuous, morally pure, or sacred. Since the day of Adam and Eve we think of ourselves as being blemished, sullied, and marred. And those of our own day who claim the mantle of perfection or near-perfection leave us wondering how they can make such a bold declaration. We simply don't believe ourselves to be holy. Whatever this word may have meant in the first century, we find it to be a hindrance to the development of our faith today.

Nor do we think of ourselves as being set apart. In fact, we often think of ourselves as "fitting in." We don't want to stick out as peculiar or strange; that would be embarrassing. We cannot be distinguished from the moral or the good people of our age. Leaders of our day use our words and we are not disturbed. It seems acceptable to us, even if the user's life is a testimony of disbelief.

To be holy, as used in your Word, means devoted, consecrated. "[We] are a chosen race, a royal priesthood, a dedicated nation, [God's] own purchased, special people, that [we] may set forth the wonderful deeds and display the virtues and perfections of Him who called [us] out of darkness into his marvelous light."*

This exalted position is not of our doing, but of your Son. It is not an honor for honor's sake, but a position created that the good news may be proclaimed wherever we might go. We are the messenger, the bearer, the truth teller not of our own wisdom and winsomeness, but of your Spirit within us.

Enable us to wear our exalted position humbly. May we always discern the difference between our value and the value of your story; between the riches of our world and the riches of your promised kingdom; between the good times of our days and the joy in our fellowship with you. Ready or not, we are a holy people, a people set apart.

In the name of Christ we pray. Amen.

*1 Peter 2:9 *Amplified Bible*

Family Days

Family

Mothers' Day

Fathers' Day

147 There comes the moment, Loving Spirit, when we are devastated by the news of a loved one's tragedy. What should our first response be? What can we say or do for our loved one and for the family members who so lovingly surround him? How should we pray?

How we wish we could say, "There, there, now, I'm sure everything will be okay." Or if we can't offer words, surely there must be something we can do. Perhaps we can locate a new specialist, a new medicine, a new diet, a new prayer — something, surely something.

Then we come back to the wall that we will never climb. Our helplessness makes us angry that we cannot find a glimmer of hope that will bring our loved one back into the mainstream of life. Even now we pray for a miracle — an extension of time, a soothing comfort — that will erase the tragedy that has been etched unwanted upon our lives.

O God, we turn to you because our need is so great. We place ourselves with those members of the faith who have stood where we stand. As they were sustained, so we wish to be sustained. While our sorrow and pain will continue, assure us that we will not be forsaken. Those members of the faith were comforted and their lives did not end in vain. They came to you and their lives were held in honor. So it will be for our loved one and us. This we claim not because we are deserving, or all-knowing, but because it is the nature of your love to sustain us, no matter what occurs.

Grant us now a glimmer of that future day when we will, in the presence of your joy, be free from disease and death. Reach through our vacillating faith with your Spirit that keeps us focused on you, the Creator of the life that never ends. Regardless of the content of our days, we place our trust in you.

In the name of Jesus Christ we pray. Amen.

Family

148 Gracious, heavenly Spirit, we come to you with a specific
need in mind — the need of persons who live alone. Within our
church and our circle of friends there are those whose mate has
died and who now no longer have the counsel and support of a
spouse. For years the chores and responsibilities were carried by
two; now they fall upon one, often one who has diminishing physical abilities and decreasing financial resources. This can fast become an imprisoning way to live.

Some of us have lost our mates by death or divorce, and now
we have the care of the children and the responsibility of a
household which requires us to work away from the home. The
demands upon us are many and available time for ourselves keeps
shrinking.

Some of us live alone by choice. It hurts when others suppose
our only motivation is to escape the marriage relationship and the
rearing of children, because we selfishly want our freedom to do
what we want to do. Lord, may our critics walk in our shoes. Living alone is not easy.

The "perks" of our society are not always available to the single
person, especially if a woman. May we proclaim that the single
person is as truly human as all others who live within the family
structure.

Others of us — for many different reasons — find ourselves
living with our children or another family member. What starts out
with high hopes can become a stress-filled home with many mis-
understandings. While this doesn't seem to qualify as living alone,
for many of us it becomes a loneliness created by the clashing of
wills spoken or unspoken.

Dear God, for those of us who live in a singular life, chosen or
unchosen, grant us your blessings as you bless all others. May our
lives be honored and given stature, first from you, then from ourselves, and finally from those who make up our circle of friends
and family.

We reach out to you for we enjoy and need your love as we need your counsel and direction. You are the source that supplies us with the good life. Your love for each of us is full — without measure — regardless of our family setting.

In the name of Jesus Christ we pray. Amen.

Family

149 How unrelenting, Holy Spirit, is your call to serve your kingdom. We thought with the approach of old age that we had fulfilled your call and would, therefore, be free of it. We aren't. It hasn't come back in exactly the same make-up as before. It is wearing a different hat, but as soon as the introductions were made we realized who it was that was bidding for our attention. What a blow to our carefully planned lives.

Why can't this disquieting call go away? Why must we deal with such unfinished business? Shouldn't younger ones step forward? Other people aren't bothered by it. It seems they're not called to task when they set aside their allegiance. Why is this weighty matter attached to us?

Please remember, O God, that we've grappled with this call to duty before. We've dedicated sleepless nights and grueling daytime hours to its resolution. At various times we believed we made progress in reaching the goal of our call — at least we achieved a partial answer. It seems we have done enough, certainly our share. We've become weary and we want to rest. Is it so bad that we ask this after months and years of struggling to succeed?

This brings us to the matter of success. Why does our work need to succeed? Do you know what a painful and impossible goal this is? A striving after perfection would be best left in the hands of others — our sons and daughters. People who have greater insight, persistence, who aren't so limited and weary as we are. Ones who are much better versed in the scriptures, who can say things better than we, who are gifted with a strength we no longer possess.

We don't know if we can say, "Yes," again. We're not sure if we fully said, "Yes," in the past. Can't we go along just as we are?

This confounded challenge, who put our names to it anyway? The proclamation, alas, is ours to give. No one else lives where we live. It is not one else's task. If we don't say, "Yes," no one else will, for at last this call is ours alone. No one else can breathe for us. No one else can beat our hearts. We shall put our hands to the task.

This we pray, in the name of him who calls us to gather the harvest. Amen.

173

Family

150   O God, the closer we draw to Jesus, the more wondrous are his words from the cross, "Father, forgive them; for they do not know what they are doing." It occurs to us that we can explain away these valiant words by reminding ourselves that after all he is God. You could expect something like this from him. But if he is flesh of our flesh, then is it expected of us to do something similar? How can this be?

You see us in court rooms, railing at those who have harmed or killed our loved ones. We search for words that will hurt the guilty, not only in this moment but for all the remaining days of his/her life. Our shrill voices carry the hatred and venom that permeates all our conscious thought. The courts and the community support our verbal spewing believing that the guilty fully deserves this acidic volley of our words.

We understand today's anger, but what of tomorrow? It is one thing to explode at the time of the criminal's sentencing, but are we to continue exploding from here on out? Who will suffer from our untamed anger? Will the criminal continue to suffer every time we vent our wrath? Or is it we — the holders of the scorching words — who will pay the price?

This brings us to the moment of considering forgiveness for the one who has brought chaos to our souls. Jesus forgave because of the need of those who brought him to death. We extend our forgiveness for the sake of the guilty and for ourselves. We cannot carry the burning acid in our stomach endlessly; we have need of neutralizing it. So let our words of forgiveness release the criminal and ourselves. May that experience of freedom be the harbinger of our citizenship in your kingdom.

We pray in the name of him who forgave us. Amen.

Family

151 We thank you, Our Creator, for the Josephs and Marys of our world. They are the mothers and fathers who care deeply about their children. They quicken our hearts, bring joy to our weary spirits, and give us hope for tomorrow. We are indebted to them for they are keeping alive the values and dreams we cherish most.

It is never easy to be a parent. It would seem that being a loving and effective parent is more of a challenge today than at any earlier time. Information inundates our homes, and how does a parent determine which is acceptable or unacceptable? How can we obtain the wisdom necessary to guide our children through all the claims and counterclaims that bid for our attention and loyalty?

How do we know when to say, "No," and when to say, "Yes"? When do we protect our children by restraining their activities, and when do we grant them freedom to experience life on their own? How do we contain the joy they bring us, without alienating our friends by the continual telling of our children's accomplishments? On the other hand, how do we keep on loving these children when they spurn our counsel, ignore the events of our lives, and smash the values that we hold closest to our hearts?

Life is difficult. Life is joy. Enable us to see you, O God, in both. You have entrusted us with your sons and daughters. What an honor! What a challenge! Thank you, Lord. Amen.

Mothers' Day

152   Our gracious heavenly King, we suspect that you grieve over the headlines that tell of mothers killing their children. These are such perverse events. We keep saying to each other, "How can a mother do such a thing?" Such reports begin to eat away at the reverence with which we have held motherhood. Subtly we begin to disvalue those who have given us birth.

Today, God, we choose to recognize the vast majority of mothers who are struggling to be the very best mothers they can be. They give careful thought to their children's diets and schedules. They make regular appointments for their offspring to see the doctor and the dentist. Toys are selected with their son or daughter's safety in mind. Vacations are planned that will bring enjoyment to their children. They anticipate their needs by purchasing clothes that will endure and lay aside money for their education or training.

They share with their sons and daughters the wisdom they have gained across the years. When life goes sour for their child, they can bring a special sensitivity and solace. Mothers learn to read their offsprings' behaviors and attitudes as a way of understanding what they are experiencing. It is their dream to supply what is needed in a given situation while being as unobtrusive as they can be. Joy is theirs when their son or daughter succeeds and matures.

There are those times when they fail to supply what is needed. They speak too quickly or use words they soon regret. Choices that seemed best at the moment, turn out to be wrong and become a burden for months and years. Hear them, O God, as they humbly face their errors and then seek your forgiveness and a renewal to prepare themselves for the days ahead.

We hold them in awe. Their devotion to the day-in and day-out tasks of rearing a family earns our abiding respect. We don't look for perfection; we look for faithfulness and we are not disappointed. In the name of Jesus Christ we offer this prayer. Amen.

Fathers' Day

153 On this Fathers' Day, O Lord, we express gratitude for those who have been our fathers in the church — Saint Paul, John, Martin Luther, the Wesley brothers, and especially for those of our own church who have been our guides and mentors.

We thank you for the founding fathers of our nation: the gallant and perceptive Washingtons, Jeffersons, Franklins, and Lincolns. We look back on their accomplishments and wisdom and can scarcely believe that we are the heirs of their work. We are most fortunate.

Thank you for our fathers. When we were children we didn't always see what they were doing in our behalf. But when we did, we gave them a childish hug or kiss — and how pleased they were.

As we grew older we became more aware of their pride in us, their joy in our successes, their pleasure in our dreams. How reluctant we were to break our childhood ties from them.

We thank you for our fathers, even when they failed to meet our needs or care for us as we had hoped. As disappointed and angry as we felt in response to their failure to love and provide for us, we now choose to cling to the good memories of those days.

We hold up to you all of us who are fathers. We have need of your wisdom. Let your love move through us to our sons and daughters. How we delight in our children and grandchildren who succeed in the drama of life. We pray that faith, hope, and love will characterize their days upon this earth.

In the name of the Holy Spirit we pray. Amen.

Fathers' Day

154 This morning, O God our Creator, we remember our fathers. For some of us our memories are joyful and uplifting. We recall a father who loved us, cared for us, aided us in our dreams and, most importantly, was always there for us regardless what took place in our lives. For others of us Fathers' Day brings feelings of emptiness and pain. In some instances it was a relationship filled with heated words and misunderstanding. And for a few of us who never knew our fathers, we wonder what might have been.

Now we are fathers and grandfathers and we wonder how we measure up. Are we too harsh or too easygoing? Are we too permissive or too bossy? Are we too calloused or too sentimental? Are we too tight or too generous? Do we hang around too much or are we too often absent?

We turn to you today that we might learn how best we can live with our children in the time allotted to us. How can a love, that often gets buried underneath all the other things we say and do, be expressed to those we so cherish and adore? We need a strong measure of courage to mount up the strength we need to speak from our hearts. If that day never comes, then may we "speak" our love through touches, hugs, presents, and smiles.

We bring to you, O God, those broken relationships that now appear to be beyond repair. Our wisdom, our reaching out, leaves us far short of reconciliation. Will you care for those whom we have failed and who have failed us. Your love is our continuing hope.

Thank you, heavenly Spirit, for all the moments of love shared with our children and grandchildren. The memory of laughter, sticky kisses, zany antics, thoughtful words, tears, and vows of love will be cherished all our days.

Please minister to us all, our heavenly Spirit. Amen.

National Days/Holidays

Memorial Day

Independence Day

Peace With Justice Sunday

Election Day

Thanksgiving

155 Today, Creator God, we remember.

We remember the courage of our forefathers who decided they could no longer bow to England's crown, so they went to war to gain our country's independence.

We remember the agony and blood-letting of that war that pitted American against American, the north against the south. Even to this day the wounds of that fighting are yet to be healed.

We remember that many years ago we sent our troops to "fight the Kaiser" in a war that was to end all wars. Then less than three decades later we returned to Europe to fight the same enemy. This time we were much more jaded about our prospects for peace.

We remember fighting in the east in the '40s, in the '50s, in the '60s, and the '70s. And recently we brought home the men and women who fought there in the '90s. We still speak of peace, but we don't know how to make it last.

We are proud of the men and women of our armed forces who have fought with such skill and bravery. We are humbled when we consider those who have been wounded, or killed, that we might continue to enjoy our freedom and our democratic way of life.

We are chagrined that for two centuries we fought and failed to establish an enduring peace. Our world neighbors, who yearn for the end of war, have also failed to find peace.

O God, in spite of our world's horrendous failures in this regard, we still cling to the dream that someday the lamb will take its rest with the lion. We search and pray for the day when we will rise above matters of race, economics, religion, territorial rights, weaponry, and political power. We want to hasten the day when we will honor others as we honor ourselves. Take our faith and mold it into a new hope for all your children of this earth.

We pray for those who have served us and serve us still.

We pray in the name of Jesus Christ. Amen.

156   Today, our Creator, we remember those who have served our country as members of the armed forces. We recall seeing their smiling faces when they returned from World War II. We remember the parades, the confetti, the shouts, the band music we offered them in appreciation of their triumph.

We remember those who fought in Korea and the frustration they experienced because they were not able to defeat the enemy because of a pre-set boundary that stopped their progress.

We also remember that we turned our backs on our Vietnam veterans, by telling them they had fought the wrong war. What a dark day that was.

Today, we honor all the men and women who have responded to our country's call. We treasure their bravery and loyalty. We also remember those who remained at home praying and working in support of our armed forces.

This hour, Eternal Peacemaker, we seek your wisdom on behalf of our country's destiny. We have known from the beginning that we've needed to respond to your truth in the conduct of our affairs and in relationship to other countries of our world. Yours is not an exclusive truth; it envelopes all people regardless of race, creed, sex, age, or ability. Strengthen us in the living of your way.

In the name of Jesus Christ, we pray. Amen.

157 What a powerful idea, Eternal God, lurks within the word independence. Think of it: we are fully in charge of our lives. We have no need to secure another's approval. We can turn right or left, go up or down, or move in our out as we choose.

What a bold, self-assured, and creative step it was when the early colonists determined to break free of England's dominance. Sometimes we romanticize the days of Thomas Jefferson, George Washington, Benjamin Franklin — not seeing the sleepless nights, the bloodied soldiers, and the shattered familial love that once held England and us together. We set out on our own course — let conventional wisdom be hung.

Independence isn't our country's exclusive province. It marks the yearning of many peoples and nations. It is the heady potion young people desire. It is the yearning of the apprentice, the understudy, the rookie, and the scholar.

It characterizes the dream of first century Israel held in the grasp of the Roman Empire. They were convinced that someday the messiah would appear and lead them to victory over their suppressors. Someday Israel would be free. Many centuries later those words would be echoed by Martin Luther King, Jr., "free at last." Is there a dream of more grandeur? Is there a more powerful desire? Is there a more universal hunger and thirst?

Moving to our independence is done with just one goal in mind — to be free! But what happens when those about us set out to reach the same goal? We run the real risk of becoming enemies. Suddenly independence is exclusive. We lose sight of freedom's meaning, when we move to block the independence of others claiming that it is ours alone.

Jesus lived and died that we might be set free. Paul claimed, "For freedom Christ has set us free."* It is the next part of the journey — beyond freedom — that vexes us. God, enable us to see beyond the narrow conviction that no one will ever tell us what to do. There is a step beyond freedom and independence — it is the step taken toward you, O God. Only as we relinquish our independence to you will we know what freedom is. We can become who we are to become only within your will.

In the name of our Master and Teacher we pray. Amen.

* Galatians 5:1 *RSV*

158 Our Heavenly Redeemer, as a country we remember and glorify our past battles and wars. We proudly display the flag from our porches; lustily sing our country's songs; proudly step-it-off in parades; happily clap our hands to the refrains of John Philip Sousa; and eagerly applaud any speaker's reference to patriotism. Despite our country's faults we remain proud of her and gladly advance her position within the world community any way we can.

We also know, Eternal Spirit, that war is not glorious. The rows and rows of white crosses in our national cemeteries, marking the graves of those who died for our country, eloquently remind us of the ugliness of war. There is something appalling about the corpse of young men or women who have had their lives snuffed out at the very time they would have begun their chosen vocation, exchanged the vows of marriage, established a home, and contributed to the life of their community and country in peaceful ways.

O God, because war is so repugnant, let us not turn away, however, from all thoughts of battle lest we dishonor those who so faithfully served to protect our way of life. We are not only grateful for those who literally gave their lives, but for those who returned home wounded or ill — and as a consequence had to accept a lesser dream, or no dream at all. We are so thankful for those who served behind the scenes in the various theaters of war, and for those who contributed to the war effort back home.

We lovingly express our gratitude to the families who gave up their sons and daughters in the service of our land. May they always take pride in the sacrifice of their loved ones.

These words we offer in the person of our Lord and Savior. Amen.

159 We know what we want to pray for, O God, but we're not sure it will do any good. What we want is world peace. So we shall pray for world peace. But we wonder if it will have any effect on the armies poised for war.

It's a little like praying that everyone in the world will be nice to everyone else this coming Tuesday. It may be a good idea, but it strikes us as having no connection or influence with the world as we know it. Forgive our blindness. But what are the chances of each of us being nice to each other next Tuesday? What are the chances for the establishment of peace? Our doubts assail us. The immensity of the conflict intimidates us.

So we begin by praying from our need. We disregard the discordant voices within us, that we might speak to you from our hearts. This is a matter of faith. Grant us courage to meet the test.

We come to you, we admit, because there is no other place to go. We have arrived at the end of the line. The whole world has become silent, waiting for what is to happen next. We pray, of course, that it will be peace.

There is no one within the world community wise enough, powerful enough to lead us to this great hope. We are the victims of our pride and our military power.

You alone can save us. We lift up to you the great leaders of the world and pray that they will heed your wisdom for the days ahead. May they — and those who work with them — be successful in finding a way to resolve this nightmarish impasse before thousands and thousands of lives are lost.

We lift up to you the young men and women, on both sides of the conflict, who have been placed at such great risk. Even knowing what will happen if war begins, we still pray for their safety. We can do no other. We pray for their husbands and wives, and for their children. We pray for their parents, their brothers and sisters, their friends. We pray for our allies. Even though it is sometimes difficult for us, we pray for our enemies. They too will twist in pain and die ignominiously upon the earth's crust.

How we yearn for peace, the reunion of families, and the resumption of tasks that are designed to meet human needs in the ways of compassion and gentleness.

Take our words, as faulty as they may be, and transform them through the power of the Holy Spirit that they may serve your purposes among all humankind.

In the name of Jesus Christ we pray. Amen.

160 Sometimes, O Sovereign God, when we look at the meagerness of our gifts and abilities, we wonder what help we can possibly bring to meet the great needs of mankind. What wisdom can we share with the Arab and Israeli nations embroiled in hostilities and disputes that go back centuries? What resources can we share with former Communist states that now try to fit themselves into a democratic way of life? What is it we can do to reverse the ways of hatred, starvation, and fear that conspire to bring thousands and thousands of people to death? Our five or ten dollar checks sent here and there — it is hoped in combination with many other similar contributions — may bring some alleviation to the world's problems.

But the battles over hatred, repressive government, and starvation aren't fought only with checkbooks. They are most effectively fought in our living rooms, school rooms, and places of worship. Here in the presence of family and friends our faith reveals those beliefs that enable us all to live in respect, honor, and protection of one another. Here we imprint our children, our educational practices, and worship activities with those values that will empower our world to achieve and sustain peace.

Our gifts, Eternal God, seem meager measured against the needs of our world, but not our faith. What you have made possible through the life, death, and resurrection of your Son overcomes even the most wretched of failures committed by your children. We do not stand alone facing the world's needs. We stand with each other and with you. Our lives are important, for we have the opportunity to witness to your nature through all our years.

This we pray in the name of your Son. Amen.

161   Now, O God, we thank you for the end of war. What a gruesome spectacle it was. What an overwhelming display of power. But what a heartache to see such confusion and fear in the faces of men whose spirits were broken. What ghastly scenes of ravaged and burned buildings and cities. Our hearts ache for those — be they ally or foe — who paid the price of limb and life. Sometimes they were a people who had little to do with the war, but by location or circumstance were compelled to pay the ultimate price.

We rejoice for anticipated homecomings. Many families will welcome their loved ones in joy and thankfulness. We can easily imagine the laughter, the kisses, the good food, and the endless attempts to put joy into word and behavior.

For those whose child, spouse, or parent will come home injured in body or spirit, we pray for healing. For those whose loved ones will not return alive, we seek lasting comfort. It may be of little solace now, but some day may pride in their loved one's sacrifice bring them serenity and a deeper peace.

We pray for the families of enemies whose suffering we likely will never know, but whose pain we can well imagine.

Let us, our Creator, prepare for the hard work of peace. Many of the problems that led to this war remain unsolved. Obstacles caused by pride and weapons of war are, for the time being, set aside, but the problems of prejudice, poverty, violence, and revenge continue. There is no international good-will fairy who can make everything right by tomorrow morning.

Our hope, gracious God, is in you. We know how deeply you yearn for peace; we also know that it may cost us more than the war. Commitment, sacrifice, forgiveness, and hope may require that we share much of what we have, as well as the energy and labor of our days. If we can succeed arm in arm with each other and with you, what a day of glory that will be! This is the dream we follow. This is the dream we dare not relinquish.

Hear our words offered through our Lord and Savior, Jesus Christ. Amen.

Election Day

162 O God, as our country moves closer to the time of elections, we are drowning in a sea of promises. We are reminded that being honest, totally honest, may be the work of a lifetime. It's so very easy to masquerade, "round off" the sharp corners, soften the harsh words, and before we consider the impact of our words, we have misrepresented the truth.

Discerning the truth is also the work of a lifetime. We listen to the candidates running for office and they seem so sincere and convincing. Yet dealing with the same events or issues, they come up with very different conclusions. So we turn to each other saying, "Who can we believe?"

Let us begin by speaking the truth to each other. Enable us to discern the truth and when we hear ourselves portraying our qualities as better than they are — grant us the grace to stop talking. When we begin to select words that will put our deeds in a better light — assist us to stop immediately and find words that will put us closer to the facts.

How we treasure friends and family members who are unfailingly honest. We know we can count on them. They are to be trusted at every turn. So we choose to be. We want those close to us to believe us. We strive to create an atmosphere of honesty and reliability.

We are grateful, God, for your honesty and truth revealed in the life, death, and resurrection of your Son. There is no deceit in you. May we be your trustworthy children.

These words we offer through the Holy Spirit. Amen.

Thanksgiving Day

163 Lord, the world around us is brimful of good things —
indeed the harvest has been plentiful. We give you thanks.

As we enter into the celebration of Thanksgiving weekend,
mindful of all that you have given, we are conscious of the inadequacy of our words to praise you. How can our "thank you's"
measure up to the greatness of your gifts?

Yet to say nothing, because of our inadequacy, would be cowardly. To mouth the words of others, because they seem more el-
evated and eloquent, only robs us of being in touch with you and
leaves us cut off from our own voice.

Furthermore, repeating old prayer formulas, as if this is something that must be done, becomes the practice of boredom under
the guise of piety. Therefore, each of us comes before you, even
with our ineffective words, to reveal our inmost thoughts of gratitude.

This morning, we lift up our collective thankfulness for the
courage and sensitivity of the early leaders of our country. Their
unquenchable thirst for freedom brought them to our shores. The
same insatiable thirst made hallowed such phrases as "worship
according to the dictates of your own heart," and "each individual
is invaluable." Their consuming delight in these reflections of freedom have become our inheritance. God, we see your hand at work
in the satisfying of their thirst.

May we in gratitude devote ourselves again to this gift offered
through our forefathers. May our nation continue to value the idea
of freedom. Greater still may we be a model of freedom so that the
world might come to experience this basic joy.

Therefore, may we lift our vision beyond the festive nature of
this weekend until our eyes come to rest on you.

In the name of our Lord and Savior we pray. Amen.

Thanksgiving Day

164 O God, we thank you for the ancient witness of your presence, so wonderfully recorded within your printed word.

We thank you for your persistent self-revelation through the people of Israel and through your Son, our Lord and Savior, Jesus Christ.

We thank you for the ingenuity of your children, but we thank you more for your insistence that your love be proclaimed so that all people can overcome the ravages of sin.

We thank you for your tender mercies made available to those who are the subject of our intercessory prayers.

We thank you for:

New opportunities and old friends;

Careful doctors and daring innovators;

Homemade solutions and mass-produced tools;

Fashionable blouses and comfortable old sweaters;

Friends who check on us and friends who don't remind us of our faults;

The brilliant colors of fall and the muted tones of spring;

Fresh fruit and canned peaches;

Loving dogs and self-contained cats;

Long letters from family and short notes from people we just met;

Strength provided by our faith and caring empowered by your love;

Endless variety of plants and trees and the greenness of grass that never wearies us;

Eternal love given us through your Son and eternal life granted us in his resurrection.

Hear our prayers of thanksgiving, our Creator and Master. Amen.

Thanksgiving Day

165   Lord, this is the time of year when we Americans remind ourselves to be thankful. Of all people on the face of the earth, surely we are the ones who have the most reason to be thankful.

We remember when we were children in Sunday School being told to offer a sentence prayer in which we were to tell one thing we were thankful for. We went around the class and no one was bypassed. You took note that we were grateful for a basketball, snow, a puppy, a new jacket that sported our school colors, hamburgers, Thanksgiving dinner, and Christmas morning. We also threw in a few things we thought our Sunday School teacher wanted to hear, like the Bible and our Sunday School class. Did you ever chuckle at our prayers?

Now, years later, we turn to the same kind of prayer. However, we like to think that we are more sophisticated. So we thank you for a balanced diet, warm clothing, and insulation that keeps the cold from our rooms. We thank you for cars that plow through the snow, music that lifts our spirits, prayers that touch our wounded souls, and health care that often borders on the miraculous.

While recent hurricanes, earthquakes, and tornados brought many death, injury, and destruction, we are grateful to see how we and our brothers and sisters of the faith responded in caring for those in such great need. These are some of our finer hours and we are grateful.

But how should we understand what our eyes and ears tell us is happening in other countries of the world? If, as a nation, as a form of government, we have faithfully held out the promise of freedom — and meant it from our hearts — then we are grateful. If as a people we share our resources of food, medicine, and technical know-how then we see your will at work and we are grateful.

May we be faithful to offer our thankfulness every day. This is our prayer offered in the name of Jesus Christ. Amen.

Index